TIME-SAVERS

GEOFFREY MOSS

The McGraw-Hill Companies

Sydney New York San Francisco Auckland
Bangkok Bogotá Caracas Hong Kong
Kuala Lumpur Lisbon London Madrid
Mexico City Milan New Delhi San Juan
Seoul Singapore Taipei Toronto

First published 2001 by Moss Associates Limited, New Zealand

Text © 2004 Moss Associates Limited
Additional owners of copyright are acknowledged on the Acknowledgments page.

National Library of Australia Cataloguing-in-Publication data:

Moss, Geoffrey 1926– .
Time-savers.

Includes index.
ISBN 0 074 71400 7.

1. Time management. I. Title.

650.1

Published in Australia by
McGraw-Hill Australia Pty Ltd
Level 2, 82 Waterloo Road, North Ryde NSW 2113
Acquisitions Editor: Javier Dopico
Internal design: Square Peg, Design & Illustration
Cover design: R.T.J. Klinkhamer
Printed on 70 gsm woodfree by Pantech Limited, Hong Kong.

McGraw·Hill Australia

A Division of The McGraw·Hill Companies

"People can be put into three categories:
those who make things happen
those who watch things happen
and those who wonder what happened."

What category are you?

About the author...

Geoffrey Moss has worked in communications and training for four decades and has conducted seminars and workshops in twenty Asian and Pacific countries.

He is a Fellow of the New Zealand Speech Board, an Honorary Fellow of the New Zealand Institute of Agricultural Science, and was an Eisenhower Exchange Fellow in the United States of America.

He was Director of Information Services for the New Zealand Ministry of Agriculture and Fisheries and Senior Planner (Agriculture and Rural Development) for the United Nations Development Programme for Asia and the Pacific, based in Bangkok.

In 1990 he was a senior lecturer at the Alafua Campus of the University of the South Pacific in Western Samoa. He is a regular training consultant to the Singapore Institute of Management.

In 1991 he was awarded the NZIAS Sir Arthur Ward Communications Trophy.

His books have been published by 22 publishers, in 16 countries and in 8 languages.

Also by Geoffrey Moss

"Ways with Words"

"Visual Ways"

"Training Ways"

"Stimulating Agriculture"

"Workbook to Stimulate Agriculture"

"The Trainers Handbook"

"Getting Your Ideas Across"

"Be An Achiever"

"Survival Skills for New Managers"

"Persuasive Presentations"

"New Horizons"

"The Trainer's Resource Book"

"Managing for Tomorrow"

"Time-Savers for Busy People"

"A Rolling Stone"

CONTENTS

If a new task is thrust upon you or you have to organise an event, use these lists and guidelines to remind you of the basic principles involved. They will make your life easier and can save you much time.

Key words have been chosen for the initial words in the title and the lists have been arranged in alphabetical order.

INTRODUCTION

The success of our book "Time-Savers for Busy People" in a wide range of countries, including China, India, Singapore and New Zealand, proves that people are searching for help to cope with the increasing pressures of modern business.

This new book has many additional topics with checklists and guidelines to act as reminders for busy people.

Work pressures continue to increase daily. There are more books, magazines, journals, newspapers and letters to read. There is more information to sort through on the Internet, more e-mail messages to answer. There are more radio and television stations competing for your time. As cities increase in size it takes longer to get to work.

At the same time there are more family pressures, more social and networking pressures. If you think you are busy now, I can assure you your life will get busier so don't let other people take control of your life.

Sound time management is the key to a successful career. Value your time. It's your most precious resource. The successful people in this world are those who can get things done quickly and efficiently. They don't let trivia and time-wasters clog their day. They plan their work so they can devote their time to their most important jobs and delegate to others as much as possible.

This simple book of checklists and guidelines was written to help you get things done more efficiently. It deals with basic principles in simple language and was written to show you how you can save time and make your life easier and less stressful. It is based on the author's experiences over more than fifty years working for private, government and international organisations.

If you have a job to do and you need a quick reminder of what is involved and how to succeed, this book is for you.

CHAPTER ONE

BE AN ACHIEVER

The most influential people in this world are the people who get things done. They are the people who have learned to manage their time successfully by creating good work habits, planning their tasks carefully, setting their priorities wisely and allocating their time effectively.

You, too, could become an achiever by following these simple rules.

GOLDEN RULES FOR GETTING THINGS DONE

1. Set a daily routine and keep to it if possible.

2. Prioritise your work for importance and urgency.

3. Fix deadlines for all important jobs and tell others.

4. Do the things which require maximum concentration when you are at your peak productive times.

5. Learn to delegate routine and less important tasks to others.

6. Plan your tasks. Think before you act.

7. Break big jobs down into manageable units.

8. Do one job at a time. Once you start a task try to complete it.

9. Plan your calls. Jot down your objective and key points.

10. Make time for relaxation and enjoyable social activities.

11. Aim for high standards, not perfection.

1 Set a daily routine and keep to it if possible

" We all have one thing in common — a 24 hour day. It's how we use our time that makes the difference. "

Experience will show you your best time for planning, for interviewing, for thinking, for networking, for writing, for making telephone calls and for walking around meeting staff and clients. If you are in doubt keep a record of your activities for a few days to analyse how you spend your time.

Start by taking one day at a time. Then each day becomes a step towards getting into a productive routine.

Once your routine is accepted by colleagues and staff you will have fewer interruptions and you will get more done.

2 Prioritise your work for importance and urgency

Set your priorities

Focus your energy on what you hope to achieve. We all have different priorities and different problems to solve.

There are two ways of setting priorities; according to urgency or according to importance.

Most people set them according to urgency and never start a project until they reach a deadline. They spend most of their time answering queries and problem solving for others.

If you are not coping because of work pressure you have three choices.

You can:

1. Work longer hours

2. Work more efficiently

3. Do only important work

1. Work longer hours

You could set aside an hour or two at the beginning or the end of each day for study or extra work. This way you may get through more work but you will probably get tired and the quality of your work could suffer.

" Don't let others manage your time."

2. Work more efficiently

You can do more work in the time available with strong discipline. You must become something of an efficiency expert, watching time, motion and deadlines. Commitments and deadlines get work done but make sure you don't overdo them or your staff relations will suffer.

3. Do only important work

This is the best approach. List your activities and set out your priorities. Perhaps you can break your tasks into 'essential', 'necessary' and 'non-essential' jobs.

Job Priorities

ESSENTIAL	NECESSARY	*NON-ESSENTIAL
Important jobs which you must do yourself.	Jobs which need to be done but which could be delegated to reliable workers.	Jobs which can be done when someone has spare time.

* Forget about the non-essential jobs; DO the essential tasks first.

Give essential jobs priority and set deadlines for their completion. Get rid of those pleasant but non-essential jobs. Delegate necessary time-consuming detailed work. Highly paid seniors are paid to think and lead, not to do mundane tasks.

 Remember

Concentrate on the most important jobs – the high-priority essential ones.

3 Fix deadlines for all important jobs and tell others

"Yes, I will have that report on your desk on Monday morning!"

" The scarcest resource you have is your time — ration it!"

Earn a reputation for being an achiever by meeting deadlines and getting things done.

If you set yourself deadlines, and tell others, you will feel more committed to achieve them.

People who get things done build a good reputation and are in demand for jobs with increased responsibilities.

4 Do the things which require maximum concentration when you are at your peak productive times

When do you work best?

Identify your peak working hours and use them wisely.

Some people are 'early birds'. They get up early and are most creative during the tranquil morning hours. The first few hours at work are peak times for some. If you are one of those don't waste this time doing routine jobs such as reading a newspaper or the mail, or making routine phone calls. Others work best late in the afternoons or in the quiet of the evening. They have been called the 'owls' and the early starters, the 'fowls'.

Are you an owl or a fowl?

Allow time to 'warm up' to creative work. Reading a stimulating book or article helps. Many people drink coffee or tea, others go jogging or walking or exercise in other ways.

Try scheduling your high-priority work for the times you work best.

Avoid too many interruptions during this period — protect your peak time.

5 Learn to delegate routine and less important task to others

Your work motto should be:

"Today I am going to work smarter — not harder!"

Concentrate on your more important tasks — your high-priority ones. Forget the non-essential ones you enjoy doing. Try delegating your less important, time-consuming tasks.

6 Plan your tasks. Think before you act

Making time to think and get organised is a sound investment and should be a part of your daily routine. Your planning will depend on your work routine and your work habits.

Some 'early birds' like to plan first thing in the morning; others prefer the end of the day. Keep your plan simple and flexible. As Murphy said, "Anything that can go wrong, will go wrong", so be prepared to adjust your timetable.

Your priorities will also change from time to time. Don't worry as long as you are heading in the right direction.

Plan each day, each week and each month.

A daily planner

Everyone should plan each day's work. Many people find it more convenient to use a small note book or a planning diary rather than an electronic note book. Keep your daily planner handy at all times.

List TODAY'S JOBS (in priority order) and in another section, JOBS TO BE DONE (with realistic deadline dates).

You can keep the note book beside your bed for ideas that come to you in the middle of the night. (Write your goals and objectives and your long term plans in it too, so you are constantly reminded of them.)

" Devote your time to the critical issues. Pay attention to the matters of importance."

An action plan

" Failure to plan is a plan for failure."

Take your high-priority essential jobs and plan what action should be taken, the time required and the dates when they should be completed.

Here is a suggested plan:

OBJECTIVE	What do you want to achieve?
TASK	What is to be done?
METHOD	How will it be done?
TIME	How many hours, days, weeks?
TARGET DATE	Date when it must be completed?

With this longer-term plan, you can decide what has to be achieved in the following week and the following month.

7 Break big jobs down into manageable units

" At the beginning there was much to do. But by whittling away the tasks became few."

Tackle jobs step by step. Here is a simple technique that can help you become an achiever — and it works every time:

"Carve big tasks into small bites and deal with only one bite at a time."

Specify what you want to do, set yourself a time limit and try to keep to it. Don't be too ambitious at the start — be realistic.

By completing one step of a difficult task you are encouraged to tackle the next step. It doesn't matter what the job is — it works. Try it next time!

Many self-made people started in a small way. They set high standards and made a success of one small business, learning from their mistakes and the mistakes of others. They finished up with a chain of shops, motels, hotels, farms or other services. One small success often leads to more successes.

8   Do one job at a time

Once you start a task try to complete it.

Don't become a 'butterfly', flitting from one job to another. Concentrate on one job at a time. Do each job well and finish it before getting on to the next.

Don't get sidetracked.

If you can sort out your priorities and do only one job at a time you make progress.

If you are working on a task and someone interrupts you, don't stop and do their job. Try being more assertive and say, 'Please come back after lunch when I have finished the job I am working on. I will help you then."

9   Plan your calls

Jot down your objective and key points.

If you spend a few seconds jotting down your objective and the key points you wish to make prior to making your telephone calls or sending your e-mail messages, your can save valuable time and make your messages clearer.

" Today's preparation determines tomorrow's achievements."

10 Make time for relaxation and enjoyable social activities

" For peace of mind ration your time."

Everyone needs recreation and relaxation. Breaks away from work allow you to return refreshed and able to make better decisions and get more work done. Those who make the worst use of their time are the first to complain about not having enough time for enjoyable activities.

11 Aim for high standards, not perfection

Never spend more time on a job than it warrants. Being a perfectionist often means becoming a procrastinator. You want a reputation for high standards but don't waste valuable time.

TIME-WASTERS

Lack of planning is probably your main enemy which stops you getting things done but procrastination, interruptions and lack of concentration are also major time-wasters.

Procrastination

Don't put off unpleasant tasks. Most of us tend to take the easy way out. We make excuses and postpone difficult and time-consuming tasks. The longer we put off a difficult task the harder it becomes. We make excuses — we are too busy, or the job is too big to start just now. The world is cluttered up with unfinished projects that have been put aside to do later.

Make an effort to do jobs when they should be done. Develop good working habits and time-saving systems. If you feel you should do a job, get on with it — otherwise you will start to worry about it.

" There is nothing more fatiguing than worrying about an uncompleted task."

Overcoming procrastination

If you have a clear mission statement, clear goals and objectives and you know what you should be doing — get started!

Break jobs into small workable tasks . Try the 'divide and conquer' method. (See page 6)

Prepare a plan for your first task.

List the steps you will take.

Set deadlines — budget your time.

Commit yourself — tell others your plan.

" Tomorrow is often the busiest day of the week."

Interruptions

You can deal with unscheduled interruptions in two ways. You can either try to get rid of them or you can budget time for them.

Your choice will depend on the importance you place on the need to listen to clients and to staff or your desire to get work done.

A friend was especially busy trying to meet a deadline for an important report. The voice from the corridor was that of a talkative client. To avoid interruptions and in utter desperation my friend crawled under his desk.

The receptionist ushered the visitor into the room.

"That's strange!" said the receptionist. *"He can't be far away. He was here a few minutes ago. Would you like to wait?"*

With that they sat down and began to talk — and talked, and talked — for nearly an hour. My numbed friend eventually emerged from his cramped quarters, very stiff and very embarrassed. He vowed it would never happen again. He would face up to his time-wasting problems and learn how to deal with interruptions.

Overcoming interruptions

" There are three things that can never be retrieved —the spoken word, time past and the neglected opportunity."

Try to eliminate interruptions or delay them so they don't interfere with your peak-time priority work.

Improve your office communications to reduce questioning from staff. Use e-mail, circular letters, newsletters, video messages, conference phone calls and meetings to inform several staff members at the same time.

Schedule meetings so staff can ask questions and discuss policy matters.

At meetings start on time, get to the point quickly and keep to the agenda.

Train your assistant to 'filter' visitors and phone calls.

Plan for a quiet period free from interruptions each day during your peak working hours.

Escape to a 'secret' quiet room to do planning and creative work.

Lack of Concentration

This is more of a personal matter. If your lack of concentration is due to worry over private problems, try to resolve them quickly.

Make an effort to concentrate on one job at a time. If you are easily distracted, remove as many distractions as possible from your surroundings.

Set yourself deadlines and reward yourself when you achieve them.

OVERCOMING YOUR TIME-WASTERS

Look for these time-wasters:

No long-term plans

No short-term plans

Unscheduled meetings

Unnecessary meetings

Too many reports

Too many rules

No priorities

No clear objectives

No current job specifications

No time plans

No deadlines

Attempting too many jobs at once

Interruptions (telephone calls and unscheduled visitors)

Poor filing system

Low staff morale

Lack of procedures for routine jobs

Failure to delegate

Filling in non-essential questionnaires

People with pet projects

Unclear requests

Lack of feedback

Lack of information

Procrastination

Too much reading

Junk mail

and so on.......... **What can you do about them?**

There is an easy way......

A   Mark your time-wasters.

B   Which ones waste the most of your time? Place them in priority order.

C   Take your number one time-waster and see what you can do to overcome it. Then move on to your next time-waster.

By tackling one problem at a time and making a real effort you will progress — it's as easy as ABC. Try it!

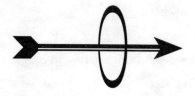

CHAPTER TWO

HELPFUL GUIDELINES AND CHECKLISTS

If a new task is thrust upon you or you have to organise an event, use these lists and guidelines to check the basic principles. They will make your life easier, and save you much time.

Key words have been chosen for the initial words in the titles and the lists have been arranged in alphabetical order of those words.

CHAPTER TWO

ACTION PLAN

ACTION PLAN

Get things done

The first step to success in any career or business is to have a plan setting out the goals and how they are to be achieved.

Similarly, in any organisation, an action plan should be prepared when a project is started or changes are to be made. It should state clearly what is to be done and how it is to be done. Ideally, it should set out the successive steps, the conditions required to complete them, and the time scheduled for each step.

A ten-point plan of action:

1   First clarify what is to be done. What changes are to be made and what results are expected? Write down in simple language what you hope to achieve. Be concise!

2   Forecast when you hope to reach your final objective. Remember things usually take longer than you think.

3   Set down the conditions and assumptions under which the work will be done.

4   Select and state the tasks needed to be carried out to complete the project. Decide who will do specific tasks.

5   What resources will be needed? Budget for these.

6   How much time will be required for the various tasks? Allow some flexibility because it is often hard to estimate the time required for some tasks.

7   Establish policies, procedures and methods of accomplishment, if required. Set goals and standards to be achieved so you will know when they have been reached.

8   Try to anticipate problems and decide how to overcome them.

9   Be prepared to modify plans as you proceed. A plan is not a static thing and changes must be made if conditions change.

10   Make sure everyone involved knows what they have to do.

" If an organisation plans to initiate a project or make changes, the best way to get people to accept them is to involve them at the planning and discussion stages."

" Failure to plan is a plan for failure."

AUDIENCE ANALYSIS ────────────

Do your research

Before you start preparing to give a speech, make a presentation, write an article or report, talk on radio or TV, make a video or film, prepare a poster or any other form of communication, find out as much as possible about your expected audience or end-user.

Composition

Who are they? Who are you aiming your message at?

Is it a small intimate group, or the mass media?

How many people are you trying to influence or entertain?

Is it a mixed audience or a specific group?

What is their average age?

What are their occupations?

What is their economic position and social status?

What is their level of education?

What are their racial backgrounds?

What do they know already?

Beliefs, attitudes and values

Will they have strong prejudices? (Consider their religious or political views.)

What are their values and accepted behaviours?

What do you think will motivate them?

If you are giving a speech or a presentation, find out why you were asked to appear. What do they want to hear? What message do you want them to take away? (See also 'Speeches', page 143: 'Lectures', page 79.)

" Eighty percent of a presentation is preparation."

AUDIENCE ANALYSIS

BORROWING MONEY

Prepare a business plan

Many new businesses fail because they are under-capitalised. It is usually easier to borrow money at the start of a new business venture than when things begin to go wrong.

Before you make your presentation to a bank or a lending institution think about the needs of the lender. Your success will largely depend on a well thought out business plan and on your reputation.

Lenders need security

They will require:

A record of your assets so they can get their money back if things go wrong.

A commitment from you.

A realistic budget allowing for all possible contingencies.

Proof of your ability to repay loans with interest.

Information you should give the lender:

" You can have a great plan and work very hard but if you can't get money when you need it, you can't get anywhere."

The reasons for borrowing the money.

The amount you need.

Your market plan.

Your price formula.

Your starting budget.

Your cash flow forecast for the next three years.

Your audited balance sheet for the last three years.

Preparing your business plan

To be objective you will need a business plan. It will help you clarify your ideas and analyse your proposed project. If you have a plan on paper you will find it easier to borrow money to buy resources. It will also help you monitor your project once you start.

If you are using your plan to raise money the document should be crisp, neat and free from errors. Put it in an attractive cover.

Make a clear statement outlining the project and its objectives. Include the reasons for borrowing the money.

Give the business history of the firm and the management staff including their qualifications and experience. Include the date of incorporation (if a limited liability company).

Give the company's financial position with audited figures for the last three years and the budgeted plans for the next three years. It should contain the names and addresses of the board, accountant, auditor, solicitor and your banker.

Describe the product or services your business will be offering and include photos if appropriate.

Summarise your market research. Give the size of the market. What competition is there? What advantages do you have over your competitors?

How do you intend to advertise, promote and sell your product and services?

Name your distributors, suppliers and sub-contractors.

State the type of premises you have or need, with the location. What are the advantages of your location?

List the equipment you have or need, and the age of your machinery, computers etc.

Describe the vehicles you have or need for transport.

Do you need planning permission or a licence to get started?

For new ventures prepare a feasibility study giving a cash flow analysis showing your predicted income and profit and loss figures.

 Remember

A business plan should be well set out, easy to read and written in the third person.

Essential financial statements

There are three main types of financial statements essential in business:

1 The profit and loss account
2 A cash flow forecast
3 The balance sheet.

Your accountant will be able to help you and advise you d' their preparation.

1 Profit and loss account

This summarises your income and expenses over a set time and should include the following items:

Income from sales or services.

Cost of goods or services sold. (Include the stock you had at the start minus the stock at the end.)

Gross profit or gross margin. (This is the difference between your sale profits and the costs of the goods or services.)

Operating expenses. (Include all your costs.)

Profit before income taxes.

Income taxes.

Net profit. (Profit or loss after paying tax.)

2 Cash flow forecast

This is a summary of the money you expect to receive and pay out during a set time — usually a year. Cash flow planning is critical to the survival of a business. It will help you forecast when you need additional funds for new equipment or additional resources for growth.

3 Balance sheet

This is a summary of assets, liabilities and your equity in the business at a specific date. It shows what the business is worth.

Presenting your case

✓ **Remember**

Try to plan unemotionally, as if you were planning for others.

Prepare a well thought out, well presented business plan, as your aim should be to persuade lenders their money is safe.

Be professional in your approach, present yourself looking well groomed, confident and full of enthusiasm.

Produce evidence of the demands for your products or services, with market surveys.

Show you have a good reputation for hard work and repayment of previous loans.

Answer questions honestly and show you have budgeted for contingencies.

Get statements to support your case from your accountant, valuer, lawyer and anyone else who can help you.

BRAINSTORMING

Generate ideas

If a group is faced with a difficult and complex problem, use a brainstorming session to help solve it.

1   Choose a leader who is enthusiastic and able to stimulate the group.

2   Start with some warm-up exercises, e.g. ask the group to list all the uses for a common object such as a brick; or you could run a competition to see who could suggest the most uses for a bucket if you were marooned on a desert island. Make it fun!

3   Make sure the group understands what is meant by brainstorming. Ask them to 'free-wheel' to get as many ideas as possible, no matter how crazy they may seem.

    Tell them there must be no comment or criticism of ideas at this stage.

4   Select one or two members to write up all the ideas on a white board, or on an overhead transparency so the whole group can see them as ideas flow.

5   Define the problem in simple terms. Probe for the real causes.

6   Set a deadline for the finish of the exercise.

7   Ask for ideas — as many as possible. The greater the number, the greater the chance of coming up with a solution. Don't allow interruptions or negative comments. Take a break as soon as enthusiasm declines.

8   After the break examine each idea to see if it has a practical application. Try putting solutions into a priority order.

9   Discuss and compare them. Look for ways to combine or improve ideas.

10   Decide on the best solution.

11   Plan how it can be put into practice and discuss implications.

" Imagination is more important than knowledge but it dies under the withering heat of criticism."

Tips

Time limits

Once your group is responding, work under pressure for limited periods of not more than forty-five minutes, preferably less.

Slow to start?

Send them off in pairs to discuss the topic before regrouping.

Keep groups small

Seven or eight participants (including the facilitator and the recorder) in each group would be ideal.

Priorities

Ideas will fall into three categories; the impossible, the unlikely and the possible. Encourage participants to choose practical ideas and prioritise them. Decide on the best solution and develop an action plan. (See also the section on Problem Solving, page 121.)

BROCHURES

Guidelines for success

If you have a product to sell or a service to offer, you will probably need a brochure to give information about it and to tell readers how to obtain it. The brochure may take the form of a booklet, pamphlet or leaflet. To ensure its success:

1   Get attention — make it eye-catching! Colour attracts attention, but the headline must be powerful and immediately interest the reader.

2   The headline must be set in large bold type. It should be clear and concise, so the reader knows what the brochure is about.

3   State your message clearly and concisely. Sell your product or service as powerfully as you can. Try to make your message interesting and exciting. What is in it for the reader? Why should they read on?

4   Emphasise the benefits. Make sure they stand out!

5   Avoid heavy blocks of type. Break them up with illustrations and plenty of sub-headings.

6   Use bullet points, numbered lists, boxes or coloured sections to break up the copy. If necessary, a design artist will set out the brochure for you so it is easy to read.

7   To give credibility to your claims, quote testimonials from satisfied customers or from well-known people.

8   Free offers should be highlighted in a special block. A sub-heading **'SPECIAL FREE OFFER!'** with an illustration draws attention.

9   Instructions on how to buy your product , or access your service, must be clear, simple and easy for clients to reply.

10 A simple form to fill in with a freepost number or freepost envelope makes replies easy to send and process.

11   Give clear instructions about how to pay if a payment is required.

12   Is there a money-back guarantee? If so, highlight it!

13   Your business address, e-mail address and website should be printed clearly on the brochure. A postal box number is inadequate because clients feel more confident if they have an address where they can contact you.

*" To catch a fish,
bait your hook
well."*

BURNOUT

Recognise the signs

We all have responsibilities. You have a responsibility to yourself. If you have a family you have a responsibility to them. You have a responsibility to your employer and to your community. If you fail to lead a balanced life and spend too much time with one at the expense of the others you will feel tired, suffer from stress and eventually burn out.

Learn to 'switch off' occasionally so you return to work fresh and creative.

Here are some burnout signs:

1   Low productivity.

2   Lack of motivation.

3   Complaining about the job.

4   Feeling depressed, resentful or helpless.

5   Worrying about family or marital affairs.

6   Dreading certain tasks.

7   Feeling tired, physically and emotionally exhausted.

8   Suffering panic attacks; being irritable and nervous.

9   Persistent headaches.

10   Lack of appetite, unable to sleep.

11   Excessive use of alcohol or drugs.

" To reduce stress, take a break, get life back in perspective and get organised!"

BURNOUT

Counsel staff

Watch for staff who show signs of physical or emotional exhaustion and be prepared to seek help for them. Mentoring, coaching and counselling all play important roles in overcoming staff burnout.

If workers show signs of burnout, here are some of the ways to help:

1   Rotate tasks so they try a variety of jobs.

2   Teach and coach new skills.

3   Allow staff to volunteer for challenging jobs.

4   Encourage creativity.

5   Allow flexible office hours and teleworking (but agreed deadlines must be met).

6   Reduce non-essential travel and non-essential meetings.

7   Reduce after-hours work and rotate after-hours schedules.

8   Delegate some of their work when possible. Distribute workloads and responsibilities fairly.

9   Allow time off or other rewards for overtime.

10   Schedule social activities and tours to promote group bonding.

11   Let staff voice their concerns. Give and receive work feedback.

12   Provide stress management programmes.

13   Encourage staff to have a proper diet and moderate exercise.

14   Thank staff for good work, as often as possible.

" Moderation in all things is the key to a balanced life."

BUSINESS

Create a competitive advantage

1 Establish explicit goals that are mutually agreed upon by both workers and management.

2 Set up effective communication systems with both staff and clients to get honest feedback.

3 Get support for change from staff and clients.

4 Counsel, train, coach and encourage your people.

5 Give individuals responsibility. Trust, confidence and accountability are the keys to success.

6 Give rewards based on results.

" *Hard-nosed competition is the best assurance of a healthy business. Aim to exceed rivals in all facets of activity.*"

BUSINESS

BUSINESS

Grow with your clients

1 Establish a good working relationship with your clients by giving them a fast, low-cost, quality service.

2 Increase the number of clients.

3 Increase the frequency of their transactions.

4 Increase the value of each sale.

5 Increase your effectiveness by improving your systems.

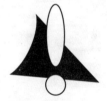

" It's the ability to deliver a consistently high quality service every time that brings clients back."

CAREER ─────────────────────

Choice

If you are entering the work force, you need to plan your career.

You need:

❖ A good basic education. Don't specialise in subjects at school too early — leave your options open.

❖ A variety of work experiences. Work in different holiday jobs; take part in work experience programmes.

❖ A variety of social experiences. Join clubs, play sports and, if possible, travel, so you meet many types of people from different social and ethnic backgrounds.

❖ Contacts. Who you know is very important.

❖ Career counselling and guidance.

❖ A plan of what you want to do and how you are going to go about it.

What are you good at ?

First identify your interests and strengths. Make four lists.

1   Your academic qualifications and your special talents

2   Jobs you enjoy most

3   Things you do best

4   Jobs you dislike doing most.

Start looking for a career that would make the best use of your qualifications, experiences and talents and has the most tasks you enjoy and the least tasks you dislike.

" The only job you start at the top is when you dig a hole."

What sort of life style do you want?

Think about the standard of living you would like and decide what you will have to do to achieve it. You may have to compromise between what you enjoy doing and your financial needs and ambitions.

Take a long-term approach

Be prepared to take a long-term approach to a career. This might involve years of study at a university or polytechnic. Join organisations that have strong training programmes and good career paths and ones which allow employees time off on salary to study. Ambitious people often have better prospects if they join large businesses or international organisations.

Get professional advice

 Remember

Look to the future. That's where you are going to spend the rest of your life.

Get advice from career counsellors — they have been trained to help you. You don't have to take their advice but they can give you leads, confirm your ideas or suggest alternatives.

Get work experience

Before you settle on a career get as much work experience as possible in a variety of jobs. Take holiday jobs in different areas and in different countries if possible. Try working in a bank, on a farm, in a shop, in an office or a factory, until you find a job you enjoy. That will give you a lead towards your career.

Overcome your weaknesses

First identify your weaknesses. If you want to set up a business and you lack the necessary skills, make an effort to learn from someone who has these skills. Go back to school, to a technical institute or to a university. Be prepared to study regardless of your age. Read books, attend seminars, join clubs to help strengthen areas you will need in your future career. For example, if you want to be a teacher you will need strong leadership and communication skills as well as technical skills. If you make up your mind and you are determined enough you will succeed.

Get your 'foot in the door'

Make the most of any contacts you have to get started in the organisation you would like to work for. If you have none, dress smartly, take your personal fact sheet and talk to the personnel manager. Ask to be put on their waiting list for future jobs. Keep in contact — don't wait for them to call you. Telephone often or call in to see if any positions are becoming vacant. Be willing to take a temporary job, a holiday job or a mundane job to get started. Work hard and show people you are ambitious and keen to work your way up in the organisation.

Don't stay in an unsuitable job

If you are not happy in your job, change it. There is always a demand for people who are talented, qualified, skilled and determined to get things done.

CAREER

Changes

A new job, a new challenge! Look at new opportunities with enthusiasm as a chance to tackle new tasks and to acquire new skills.

Don't live in the past. Keep looking ahead to the future.

Try conducting an honest self-appraisal of your work styles and people skills. You have a chance to start afresh.

Be decisive.

Practise common courtesies.

Broaden your horizons by study, travel and new experiences.

Accept change and less security as a part of today's business life.

" Nothing ventured nothing gained."

CAREER

Advancement

First get to know your corporate culture.

Find a mentor to counsel and advise you on your career steps.

Get honest feedback and monitor yourself. Don't resent helpful criticism.

Promote yourself. Don't be too modest.

Know when to stop talking and when to listen, especially when the boss is talking.

Maintain high ethical standards and a good work output.

Build good relationships and alliances. Join organisations and make an effort to strengthen your social and business networks.

Use all the brains you have and all the brains you can borrow.

Continually learn new skills.

" What you want to be is more important than what you are."

CHANGE

CHANGE

Plan for growth

Change in any organisation is healthy if it is in the right direction. A leader's job is to explain the need for change and to help people overcome their fear of it. When people recognise the need for change they are more likely to support it. They will also support what they help to create so get them involved in planning changes.

The graveyard of business is littered with organisations that failed to recognise the need to change.

The starting point for bringing about change in any organisation, regardless of size, is a draft **strategic plan**. It should involve the following:

1 A vision, mission or policy statement.

2 Setting goals.

3 Carrying out an environmental scan.

4 Carrying out a situational audit.

" First ponder, then dare."

5 A SWOT analysis.

6 Setting objectives.

7 Planning tasks to be done.

8 Preparing an action plan.

1 Vision, mission or policy statement

This should define the ambitions of the organisation and should be stated clearly and concisely in writing so everyone in the organisation knows what they are.

It should be specific and focused on the principal reason for the existence of the organisation. It must take a long term perspective and be inspirational for the teams — and give them something to aim for. They should take a pride in working towards the vision.

" To make it easier and cheaper for all people in this country to keep in touch and improve their quality of life."

For example, a telecommunication company's mission statement might be:

" To make it easier and cheaper for all people in this country to keep in touch and improve their quality of life."

2 Goals

A goal is your desired result. It is like the destination of a journey — the end of your effort.

For example, your goal or aim may be:

" To be the best company of its kind in this country, setting standards that all others strive to reach."

Goals are often hard to measure but people know when they have been achieved.

3 Environmental scan

This involves investigative research and should tell you what's going on around you.

What competition do you have?

What are your competitors doing?

What future international developments can be predicted?

How will changes in the exchange rates influence the business?

Could a change in government policies have an influence on the business? ...and so on.

4   Situational audit

Take a hard objective look at your organisation. You must be honest and completely objective! Bringing in an outsider to help has advantages. Ask leading questions. What do you do best? What could you do better? What do customers really think about your service? How can you give clients a better service? How can you cut waste?

These questions allow you to carry out a SWOT analysis.

5   SWOT analysis

Make up a list of the organisation's

Strengths, Weaknesses, Opportunities and Threats.

Make the most of your opportunities and strengths, overcome your weaknesses and head off your threats.

6   Objectives

Set realistic objectives which can be measured. An objective is more specific than a goal. A good objective should define the conditions to be met or the exact target to be achieved by a certain time.

SMART objectives should be:

Specific, Measurable, Achievable, Realistic and completed on Time. For example:

"To streamline office procedures and reduce office staff by 25% within the next six months."

7   Tasks to be done

Prepare a list of tasks needed to meet your goals and objectives.

Divide big tasks into small parts and deal with only one part at a time.

8   Action Plan

Draw up a simple action plan. How will you involve your people in this exercise?
Who does what by when? How will you keep a check on developments?

Teams with a shared vision can be very effective in accomplishing complex tasks. Get your people involved and with their help draw up simple action plans. Authority to make decisions and to act should be delegated nearest to the point where the facts are known and the action takes place. Delegate responsibility and accountability!

The vision goes downwards and the action plans and the reporting flow upward.

Plans must be reviewed on a regular basis. A plan is not a static thing — it's dynamic and changes must be made to respond to a changing environment.

Keep asking 'WHY' and 'HOW CAN WE DO BETTER?'

 Remember

To improve is to change; to aim for perfection is to change often.

CHANGE

CHANGE

Overcome resistance

People resist change for a number of reasons. Many workers fear the unknown. Will they still be employed after changes are made? How will the changes affect their work?

Some workers do not trust the motives of management. They do not understand the need for change and resist the changes.

To help reduce resistance when making changes

1   Be frank and honest about the need for the planned changes. Discuss and consider possible adverse effects.

2   Involve staff in planning, implementing and evaluating change policies.

3   Ask innovative people, who do not resist change, to support you and help explain the benefits.

4   Build up trust by talking to staff and giving them all the facts. Be enthusiastic about the changes, but listen carefully to their concerns.

5   Consider any criticisms of the proposed changes.

6   Decide on the action to be taken and reassure staff that their concerns have been considered.

7   Test the changes by running small pilot projects to show that any fears are unfounded.

8   Start by selecting one project that has a good chance of success. Then proceed gradually with the other changes.

9   When changes are made, report regularly on progress.

10   Reward people who suggest helpful changes.

"Once trust is lost it is difficult to win back."

11   Aim to make constant improvements. Change is a dynamic process so act on constructive feedback and helpful suggestions.

COACHING

Establish a rapport

Good coaches establish trust and a rapport with the people being instructed. They should encourage with praise, build confidence with graduated experiences and give honest and constructive feedback.

Hints for coaches:

1   Make sure your people know what is expected of them and explain the possible rewards for achievements.

2   Challenge them with graduated step by step experiences to build up their confidence.

Remember it is harder to unlearn bad habits than to learn new procedures.

Be patient with your explanations.

3   Arrange for systematic on-the-job coaching.

4   Give regular reports and feedback on progress. Feedback is the key to improvement.

5   Any criticism should be constructive and given in a non-threatening, helpful manner.

Praise good work publicly; criticise privately.

6   Reward effort and achievements.

"Returns from learning should be more earnings".

7   New skills must be put into practice soon after they are learned or people become frustrated.

" Increased profits are the reward of sound coaching."

COMMUNICATION

Transfer messages in different ways

Most people have too few tools in their communication kit. There are many ways to get messages across to staff, clients or the public.

Before you start, analyse the people you are trying to reach with your message . Be specific. Find out where they get their information from and aim your message at them using a scatter approach, with different media tools.

Try different ways to get your message across. Have you considered some of the following?

Advertisements in newspapers and magazines

Advisory boards, sub-committees or working parties

Almanacs

Alumni newsletters and activities

Anniversary books or brochures

Annual reports

Attitude surveys on policies, procedures, plans and practices

Badges or cuff-links

Balloons with messages

Banners

Billboards

" Be different from other people — use your imagination."

Birthday greetings

Booklets offering services or information

Books

Brochures

Bulletin boards for brief topic information

Bulletins for announcements

Bumper stickers

Bus or train advertisements

Calendars setting out events

Calling systems to locate staff (intercoms)

Campaigns

Car stickers

Cards (business, identification, visiting)

Cartoons

Charts

Circulars in 'please-take-one' containers

Civic activities

Clubs for recreation or social activities

Coasters or paper table mats with messages

Comics

Committees

Compact discs

Computer letters or messages

Conferences

Contests (art, photographic, games, puzzles, quizzes, raffles, sales, writing, model making)

Counselling sessions

Cup messages on drinking cups

Debates

Demonstrations

Diagrams

Diaries with quotes and facts about the organisation

Dictionaries

Digest or articles, statements or reviews

Direct mail

Directories (employment, services, products, telephone)

Discussion groups

Displays

Educational souvenirs

E-mail messages

Emergency cards or stickers

Exhibits (preferably active exhibits)

Eyeglass wipers containing a message

Facsimile messages

Fact cards — with a calendar on the back

Family activities — visit the factory, the office, sports day, picnic etc.

Field trips

Films

Financial reports

Floor plans

Forums

Glossaries of terms

Grapevine

Graphs, pie charts etc.

Grievance box

Handbooks for visitors and new employees

History of the organisation

Hoardings

Holiday greetings — cards or booklets with travel tips

Identification cards

Induction programmes

Information reading racks

Inservice training

Internet

Interviews

Invoices with message slips

Leaflets

Lectures

Letters

Letters to the editor

Libraries

Magazine articles and advertisements

Magnets for refrigerator messages

Manuals setting out procedures

Maps showing locations of services, buildings, parks etc.

Meetings

Memos

Menu cards or place mats

Motion pictures or videos

Museum displays

Name plates, vehicles or desks

Newsletters

Newspaper articles or advertisements

Neon signs

Notebooks with logos and information

Open-house programmes

Organisation charts

Overhead projection transparencies

Panel discussions

Paper pads with logos and commercials

Paper serviettes with messages

Pay cheques, with message slips

Pay envelopes with message or token gifts

Pens with logo or messages

Photos with captions

Picture books

Postcards

Posters

Press releases

Programmes for events such as concerts or sports days

Public address systems

Radio — interviews, commercials, news items, releases

Readership surveys

Reception activities

Receptionist and reception area displays

Reports

Reprints of articles

Rubbish bag advertisements

Rules books, lists of regulations, procedures, acts

Rumour box or rumour board

Samples of products

Sandwich boards

Seminars

Service clubs

Signs

Skits

Slogans

Social activities for staff and clients

Souvenirs with logos

Speeches

Stickers for windows, car bumpers, coat lapels

Suggestion prizes for good ideas

Symposia

Taxi advertisements

Tea towels

Teleconferences

Telephone directories, yellow pages

Telephone messages, interviews, surveys, conference calls

Television, advertisements, interviews, documentaries, news items

Theatre screen advertisements

T-shirts

Tours of plant, office, gardens, research stations

Training activities

Tuition and coaching programmes

Vacation kits, maps, first aid, sewing, insect repellent, sun screen cream

Video-television, teletext messages

Visits

Washrooms — messages above hand basins, on back of toilet doors

Whiteboards

Workshops....and so on.

COMPETITION

Beat your rivals

Learn as much as you can about organisations competing with you for supplying services or products. Aim to exceed them in all facets of activity such as quality, price, speed and servicing.

Appreciate your competitors — they are your stimulus for change. Hard-nosed competition is the best assurance of a healthy business.

Here are ways to help beat the competition:

1   Constantly research your markets and react swiftly to changes.

2   Invest in new equipment and new technologies.

3   Set up strong alliances.

4   Build up effective teams.

5   Get the best financial advice you can afford.

6   Price goods and services at competitive rates.

7   Get staff focused and involved.

8   Aim to continually improve customer services.

9   Encourage client and staff feedback.

10   Invest in training for results. Staff should be multi-skilled.

11   If possible pay by the job not the hour.

" Concentrate your strengths against your competitor's weaknesses."

COMPLAINTS

Deal with grievances fast

Businesses are successful only if their customers and clients are satisfied with the product or services. Valued customers could be lost if complaints are not handled skilfully and quickly.

Successful managers know that it is easier and more profitable to generate additional business from existing customers than trying to find new ones.

Complaints should be treated as indicators of potential trouble, so train your staff to deal with complaints promptly.

1 Be polite and helpful. Show you are concerned and willing to assist the complainant.

2 Find out precisely what the customer is complaining about. Listen carefully and ask questions. Don't make any hasty judgements.

3 Investigate the problem as soon as possible. Is it due to faulty materials, poor assembly, poor servicing of machinery, rude or inconsiderate staff or lack of training?

4 Contact the customer promptly and tell them what you have found out about their problem.

5 Discuss how to resolve the problem and what action you will take. Then act immediately - not tomorrow, not next week but NOW!

6 Surprise the customer with a gift or a discount. If you want to retain customers, do something special for them instead of just fixing the problem.

" Satisfied customers are one of a company's greatest assets. "

7 Take corrective action. Make sure the problem does not occur again.

CONFERENCE or CONVENTION

Plan and organise thoroughly

Before you start organising a conference or convention, answer these questions:

1 Why is the conference being held?
2 What are the aims of the organisation and the objectives of the meeting?
3 Who do you hope will attend?
4 How many people will you be able to accommodate?
5 What is your budget?

Your working committee

If you are the organiser your job is to coordinate activities.

Don't try and do all the work — delegate jobs to others.

Select your working committee carefully. Pick people who have the time and the ability to get things done.

Call a meeting of these people and if they agree to take a responsibility, give them instructions in writing.

> " Mr Williams. You are responsible for all publicity. Your job is to... You have the authority to set up your own working party and to delegate jobs to others. You are responsible for seeing things get done and reporting progress at the meetings of the organising committee."

Consider the theme

What is your theme?

Know what topics you want discussed.

> " Success of a conference can be measured by the level of discussion and the action that follows."

Choose the speakers

Know how speakers will perform on these topics.

Will they be compatible with your audience?

Will they be drawcards?

Contact the speakers

Phone first to see if they are available and to answer their initial questions. Follow up with a letter confirming dates, times, subject, transport and accommodation arrangements.

Prepare the programme.

Book meeting rooms.

Book accommodation for speakers and guests.

Arrange publicity. (Newspapers, television, radio, brochures etc.)

Brief and invite reporters.

Arrange catering.

Organise signs, decorations.

Arrange for a sound system.

Organise visual aids, projectors, screens and emergency equipment.

Check on availability of seats and tables.

Organise registration staff and facilities.

After the event

Write to thank speakers.

Pay accounts.

Evaluate conference and make a note of changes for next time.

Write reports.

Get follow-up publicity by supplying the media with stories and photographs.

CONFIDENCE

Build your self-esteem

If you believe in yourself you can achieve what you want out of life. So decide exactly what you want and then with determination and persistence, set about reaching your goals.

Your first step is to build your confidence.

Accept new challenges and master new skills.

Make time to continue with study, learn different skills and languages, and read widely.

Join self-improvement organisations such as debating clubs, theatre groups, lodges or Toastmaster clubs.

Participate in sports and help with any administrative jobs as well as social activities. Adventure activities such as mountaineering, rock-climbing and sailing are great confidence boosters.

Take new responsibilities. Accept office in an organisation such as a religious group, a political party, a sports club or a social group.

Help in community projects. This is a good way of getting to know people and building your self-confidence while helping others.

Try new things - new hobbies, new sports, new foods, new environments. Travel is a good way to build confidence

Keep learning and mastering new skills.

Become what you are capable of becoming by being more self-reliant and determined.

If you have confidence in yourself, others will have confidence in you. Doubt others but never doubt yourself.

"When your confidence increases your competence increases."

CONFLICT

CONFLICT

Avoid clashes

Conflict is a normal part of life caused by such things as personality differences, jealousies and poor communications. Most conflicts result from misunderstandings.

Here are things you can do to help reduce day-to-day conflicts:

1   Keep people better informed of developing situations and proposed actions.

2   Be honest and straightforward with people. If you are not happy about a situation say how you feel and say why there is a problem.

3   Confront your problems. Don't run away from them. Face up to developing situations. Don't resign from a committee or an organisation because you have a disagreement. Face up to the situation and see what you can do to bring about change. Never sulk because you didn't get your way or your ideas were not accepted.

4   Action speaks louder than words. Never make a promise you cannot keep or people will resent you.

5   Involve antagonists in planning and decision making and you will help resolve potential conflicts.

" Anger is one letter short of DANGER!"

6   Never favour some people and denigrate others. Never favour one sex against the other, or the young against the old, or favour friends and family against others.

7   Don't embarrass people by criticising them in public or make fun of them or their ideas.

8   When there is an important issue to be faced never change the subject or move the discussion to another topic. This can annoy both parties.

9   Avoid name-dropping to support your arguments.

CONFLICT ————————————————————

Resolve differences

Deal with minor disagreements quickly.

"A small leak can sink a great ship."

Here is a sequence worth following next time you need to resolve a conflict:

1   Define the conflict, from both sides' point of view.

2   Analyse the real situation. Talk about your feelings and personal reasons for the differences. Consider historic reasons. Be honest and frank.

3   Emphasise common concerns and points of agreement.

4   Make a list of possible solutions to resolve any differences.

5   Examine and discuss all the alternatives.

6   Break complex issues into workable components.

7   Be prepared to compromise and to select the best alternatives.

8   Plan the action and the sequence required to implement a policy that will resolve the differences between parties. (Who will do what, by when?)

9   Meet periodically to examine results and make changes if necessary.

" Don't concentrate on looking for differences; look for common ground."

CURRICULUM VITAE (C.V.)

CURRICULUM VITAE (C.V.)

Your personal fact sheet

The first thing you should do when applying for a job is to prepare your personal fact sheet called your curriculum vitae, your c.v. or your résumé.

It should be typed neatly and well set out on good quality bond paper. Employ an experienced typist if necessary.

Keep it simple and as short as possible. Attach a recent photograph — one where you are smartly dressed.

Attach photocopies of appropriate certificates and references.

Your c.v. should contain the following information:

Full name and address

Telephone number — day and night

Nationality

Age, date and place of birth

Educational qualifications

Work experiences

" Those who do not hope to win have already lost."

Dates, name and address of employers, type of work, your responsibilities and accomplishments.

Vacation work.

Voluntary community work.

Give details of skills relevant to the job you are applying for, e.g. computer, shorthand, or foreign language skills.

Hobbies, sports and interests

Leadership experiences in sport, youth groups, community projects etc.

Give names, addresses and phone numbers of three people who can supply references. (Be sure to contact these people first to get their permission.)

CUSTOMERS and CLIENTS

Concentrate on satisfaction

Today modern management practices concentrate on improved performance but they should concentrate more on customer satisfaction. Most customers have a choice of providers. Unless your service is in their best interest they will go elsewhere.

Customer service is the responsibility of the whole organisation. It may take weeks to find a good customer, but only seconds to lose one. Your customer relations are only as strong as your weakest employee.

What you want and what your customer wants may not be the same, but unless you give them what they want, you won't get what you want.

Ways to improve customer services:

1   Make everyone in your organisation responsible for customer and client services.

2   Take special care in selecting and training front-line staff, especially receptionists and telephone operators.

3   Try to see your organisation through the eyes of your customers. (If you were a customer would you do business with your organisation?)

4   Change your organisation into a user friendly business.

5   Get your customers and clients involved in creating the service they want. Involve them in your planning so they feel they have a stake in your organisation.

6   Develop a feedback system with your clients. (You will reap rewards if you encourage criticism and correct weaknesses.)

7   Take the time to talk to your customers about day-to-day affairs; they will tell you how you can give a better service.

8   Don't let your rules ruin relations with clients. Use common sense and be flexible with situations. Be prepared to make changes according to the situation and client needs.

9   Try to make your customers and clients feel good about themselves and their decisions.

If you can deliver a friendly, quality service, at a realistic price, you will build customer loyalty.

" If you don't take care of your customers someone else will."

DECISION - MAKING

DECISION - MAKING

Make sound assessments

Indecision can be the worst mistake some people make. Aim to make sound decisions after you have studied the topic and thought about all the consequences.

Remember many decisions are easy to make but hard to implement.

- Avoid making snap decisions.
- Don't make important decisions when you are under stress.
- Give your full attention to important decisions.
- Assess the situation fully after you have collected all relevant facts.
- Try to balance an intuitive hunch with sound logical analysis.
- Examine alternatives closely before making a decision.
- Make use of policy guidelines and past experiences.
- Consult people whose judgement you trust.
- Consider the possible outcomes when making a decision. Ask what can go wrong. Try to anticipate future developments and any changes in the situation.
- **Keep asking "WHAT, WHY, WHEN, WHERE, HOW and HOW MUCH?"**
- Consider people, profits, conflicts, materials, machinery, methods and the environment.
- After weighing up the implications be prepared to take risks.
- Once you have studied the situation fully, make your decisions fast.

" It is easier to make a decision and do something, than to worry about it."

DELEGATION

Reduce your workload

You delegate jobs:

(a) To have more time for important jobs

(b) To train staff

(c) To test staff in different situations.

If you delegate to reduce your workload, match the staff to the jobs you want them to do.

How to delegate:

1   List your tasks.

2   Mark your essential tasks.

3   Decide which jobs take up too much of your time.

4   Mark the tasks you do not really need to do.

5   Delegate as many as you can.

6   Decide who should receive these tasks.

7   Make sure they have the skills and the time.

For successful delegation:

1   Make sure the task is achievable.

2   Explain why the job is important.

3   Give clear instructions. If they are complex write them out in simple English.

4   Give the staff authority to act.

5   Tell staff what results you want.

6   Agree on a deadline.

7   Make sure they know who to go to for help, if they need it.

8   **Don't interfere** while they are doing the job.

" The ability to delegate is the mark of a good manager."

 Remember

Delegation means delegating responsibility, authority and accountability.

DELEGATION

9   Ask for feedback and regular progress reports.

10 Be helpful and positive when you receive the reports. Counsel the staff if necessary.

11 Praise good work.

Promoting the task:

1   Highlight the challenges.

2   Express your faith in their ability to rise to these challenges.

3   Tell them how the experience will benefit them.

4   Set clear performance standards — not the methods to be used.

5   Give them a model to measure their performance against.

6   Give them time to think about the task and to ask questions.

✓ *Remember*

If you are unable to delegate you have the wrong team about you.

DICTATION

Start slowly

When work pressure builds up, you can save time by dictating letters and reports. Getting started is hard.

Here are some tips to help:

Make sure you have all the relevant papers before you start.

Make brief notes for the replies you intend to dictate. See that your notes are in logical order.

Try to put yourself in the position of the person receiving the letters.

Avoid interruptions as much as possible — divert telephone calls, for example.

Treat your stenographer with consideration. Explain the nature of the work, the type of document you require, how urgent it is and whether you require a draft. Encourage the stenographer to ask questions.

Start by dictating short letters. Use full notes until you gain confidence.

Go over each sentence mentally, before you dictate it. It must sound right to the ear. Pretend you are actually speaking to the person you are writing to. Avoid slang and jargon.

" Communication must be a two way affair."

Speak clearly, exaggerating the pronunciation of words. Spell proper names and technical terms. Be considerate — don't dictate quickly. Try to keep up a constant speed with an occasional rest. Don't mumble with your hand in front of your mouth. Don't talk when eating or chewing.

Try not to interject with asides or walk around the room when you dictate.

Indicate the end of each paragraph.

If you have papers for the stenographer place them in the same order that you dictate.

Specify the people who are to receive extra copies of the document, who is to sign the correspondence and give designation.

Ask for a rough draft only if you plan to alter or revise letters.

DISPLAYS and EXHIBITS

Arouse interest

Displays and exhibits must get their messages across quickly. They should arouse interest, stimulate thought and cause action.

Guidelines for a successful display:

1 Specify your aim. What do you want your viewers to do?

2 Catch your audience's attention with a gimmick.

3 Try to get people involved — competitions are good.

4 Tell them your message. Keep it simple and crystal clear — in basic English. The fewer words the better.

5 Use mainly visuals to tell your story. Keep words to a minimum.

6 Leave plenty of space — crowded and cluttered exhibits discourage people.

7 Make any lettering large enough for people to read easily from a distance.

8 Keep the exhibit fresh and looking clean and tidy.

9 Persons looking after an exhibit should be neat and well groomed, enthusiastic and helpful. They should be replaced regularly to prevent them getting tired or bored.

10 Give a handout to people who are interested. (Simple, useful gifts are good reminders of your products or services.)

11 Make follow-up calls to people who show interest and want further information.

" If you don't stop them — you don't sell them. "

DISPLAYS AND EXHIBITS

E-MAIL

Use it wisely

E-mail is a good business tool for breaking down barriers, enhancing international understanding and for making quick decisions.

Don't let the servant become your master. Take control and use it to your best advantage. Take care you do not send off messages you later regret sending because of misunderstandings.

Some people become addicted to using e-mail and are lazy or reluctant to speak to people face to face. Talking to people and having open discussions is still the best way to get your ideas across and influence people.

Tips when using e-mail:

1   Clear your e-mail messages every day.

2   Handle them quickly. As soon as you read a message decide to:
> delete it
> act on it
> pass it on
> save it for reference
> or file it for later action.

3   Set up an efficient e-mail filing system.

4   Use message filters, the address book, templates and an automatic signature.

5   Use e-mail's reply feature to respond swiftly.

6   Plan what you are going to say before you reply. Jot down key words or phrases and put them in a logical order. Put your main idea first.

7   Write the way you would talk. Use simple words to avoid misunderstandings.

8   Do not use slang or jargon.

9   Send only 'need-to-know' information.

10 Avoid attaching extra files

When you e-mail foreign countries:

- Plan your message

- Set out your messages for ease of reading. Use headings.

- Keep your sentences and your paragraphs short.

- Be concise and clear with your messages and be considerate of the recipient's time.

- Be explicit. Use simple words and active verbs - if possible words with only one meaning.

- Remove all metaphors where things are not meant to be understood literally e.g. 'time flies' meaning time passes quickly.

- Don't use slang or local jargon.

- Use international English (or the language spoken in the country you are e-mailing, if you are fluent in it.)

- Answer all questions in detail; don't take anything for granted.

- Express figures in words and spell out dates in full, especially if you are e-mailing the United States of America.

- Finally, before you send your e-mail, proofread it. Remove surplus words and check spelling. Don't trust your spell checker; it's only an aid.

" Write succinctly and to the point and reply to incoming messages as soon as possible."

FACSIMILES

Save time and money

Messages sent by facsimile (fax) have advantages over telephone messages. They are usually cheaper, they imply urgency and they provide permanent copy. The same message can be sent to many addresses and the fax machine can also send illustrations, diagrams and photographs. Many people prefer them to e-mail because you get a hard copy.

Tips for using a fax machine:

If you are using a new machine for the first time, study the manual and make sure you know the correct way to insert the paper.

Preset your machine for no more than two 'redials'. If you are not getting through, the lines could be overloaded, so wait and try later.

Put the date at the beginning of your message. Indicate the number of pages you are sending.

Define your subject precisely with a bold heading.

Make the message as short and as clear as possible.

If any documents are torn, repair them and photocopy before you send them.

If your copy is faint, photocopy to darken it, or set your machine to low contrast.

Use 'half-tones' for better reproduction of photos and drawings.

Check the fax number, name and full address of the recipient. (Wrong numbers are costly if you are calling internationally.) Commonly used numbers should be stored in 'auto dial' to reduce the possibility of mistakes.

Check your name, address, telephone number and fax numbers and e-mail address.

Read your draft for clarity and omissions. Check for logic. (If it's an important message, test it out on a colleague to see if it is clear.) Use global English for international calls.

Spell out details. Don't take things for granted. Use simple words and short sentences.

" Get attention at the beginning of your message."

FACSIMILES

Repeat important figures in words.

Type or print your message. Hand-written messages are often hard to read.

Advise contacts if you change your fax number.

To save money:

Use simple letterheads with outlines. Don't use bold, blocked logos.

Don't use thick lines.

Keep your messages as short as possible.

Use abbreviations if the meaning is clear. e.g. &, @ etc..

Don't put your address or a commercial at the bottom of your paper. If you have a short message you will be charged for the white space between your message and your address.

If you have information on only half the page, cut the page and send only half.

You can reduce international toll costs by using a 'delayed send' to take advantage of cheap off-peak rates.

Keep your activity slips in a logical order. Use them to check your account.

FEEDBACK

Aim for continuous improvement

Feedback should be encouraged and developed as it can serve as an early warning system for problems and grievances. Encourage and welcome constructive feedback. Take care you do not discourage feedback by becoming defensive if you are criticised.

The key to success is to aim for continuous improvements and feedback can play an important role.

"Don't be defensive — encourage feedback!"

Ways to stimulate feedback:

Use social and informal functions to get feedback.

Make time to establish a rapport with people before you ask direct questions.

Learn the art of asking direct and open questions. (See 'Questions', page 127.)

"What did we do right?" "What did we do wrong?" "How can we do better next time?"

Set aside regular times for feedback sessions.

Learn to use silence to stimulate comment. Pause and wait in silence. This will normally prompt someone to express an opinion.

" Don't look for acclamation, look for constant improvement."

Watch for body language. People tend to say what they think you want to hear, but often their body language can give you a clue to their real feelings.

Ask for feedback as soon as possible after an event. *"Tell me, what did you think of the meeting?" "What improvements should we make next time?" "What did our clients think of that presentation?" "How can we do better next time?"*

Thank people for their feedback. Praise will stimulate further feedback.

Exit interviews, if well handled, can be a good source of feedback.

To give feedback

People will not achieve to their full potential unless they know what is expected from them and how they are performing. By learning to give good feedback you can improve staff performance and organisational performance.

Some guidelines to consider:

Focus on the things that can be changed.

Share your feelings and give specific examples. e.g. *"I was a little disappointed the way you spoke to that customer. Next time you have that problem I suggest you try to handle it this way ...."*

Give feedback as soon as possible after an event.

Match the feedback to the personality of the person. Some people welcome feedback, some resent it. Be diplomatic and be constructive with your suggestions.

✓ *Remember*

Criticism, like rain, should be gentle enough to nourish a person's growth.

Focus on successes rather than on mistakes. Always be specific with examples of both, but praise is the most effective for getting feedback.

Any constructive criticism you make should contain reasons for change and practical recommendations.

FINANCIAL SUPPORT —————————

Seek a grant

Trustees of philanthropic trusts are usually very busy people. If you represent a worthy organisation and want to apply for a grant, your application should be brief, clear and factual. Explain the purpose of the project, how the money will be spent and who will benefit.

Follow these guidelines to present a persuasive case for financial support:

Be positive

Enthusiasm for your project is the key to success. If you believe in your proposal and start with a positive attitude your chances of success are good. Think positively, talk enthusiastically and write persuasively.

First do your homework

Ask the funding agency for a copy of their standard application form and ask for an example of a successful application showing their preferred layout. Conform to their requirements and you will save yourself a lot of time and increase your chance of success.

" Few things can replace enthusiasm, persistence and determination of purpose."

Plan your project in detail. Prepare a brief but comprehensive statement of the nature of the project, its purpose and its importance. Where will it be carried out, who will carry it out and who will benefit?

Then make a full list of the things you need and the estimated costs. Work out a timetable for carrying out the proposals. Obtain details of the experience and the background qualifications of the people involved in carrying out the plan

Prepare your proposal

1   Your title page

It should be well set out and explicit. For example:

Use headings like: PROPOSAL TO ESTABLISH...
AT...(place)
SUBMITTED TO...
ON...(date)
BY... (name and address and contact details)

2 Purpose or objective

Describe briefly and clearly the purpose of your project. Why is it important? Who will benefit? How will you know when it has been successful?

3 How will the project be carried out?

Explain the procedure and the costing.

4 Who will carry out the project?

Give names, qualifications and experience.

5 Contacts for further information

Supply full names, addresses and phone numbers of officers and details of the organisation. Enclose a brief history of the organisation and its achievements and a list of names and qualifications of distinguished officers and trustees. Send a copy of your last annual report and audited accounts.

6 Add a list of referees

Name people who will vouch for the project and its personnel.

7 Provide a timetable

State the proposed commencement date, when the various stages will be finished and the estimated time of completion of the project.

8 Prepare a budget

Show the total cost of the project. Supply a full estimated breakdown of costs — wages, equipment, travel etc. Include the cost of an evaluation and a final project report.

State how much money and resources your organisation can contribute, and how much extra money is required.

9 How are you going to evaluate and report results?

What will be the expected impact of the results? Use objective criteria to measure results. To ensure your credibility, ask an outside organisation to design and carry out the evaluation. (Don't forget to budget for this item.)

10 Appearances are important!

Proposals are partly judged on layout and general appearance. Present your case on good quality bond paper. Double space your proposal leaving wide margins and plenty of white space. Use headings and sub-headings for ease of reading. Present your submission in an attractive cover.

HIRING STAFF ———————————————

Select the best

Time and effort are needed to select the best candidates to fill key positions. It can be expensive if you select a person who does not meet your long-term expectations. Staff morale can suffer if you make a bad appointment so start organising for staff selection well before the interview stage.

Before you start recruiting, ask the following questions:

• Are we expanding, diversifying or cutting back our operations?

• Do we really need to fill the position?

• Can we reorganise so we don't need to recruit?

• Can we use part-time or contract workers?

• Can we retrain someone within our organisation for the job?

• Have we updated the job description and planned for future developments?

• What special qualities, qualifications and skills are needed?

• Have we written a person specification?

The main steps in recruiting and selecting staff.

"You are only as good as the people you employ - their performance is your reputation."

1. Write a job description considering future developments within the organisation.

2. Prepare a person specification.

3. Advertise to find suitable applicants.

4. Prepare for the interview.

5. Interview candidates.

6. Decide on the best candidate. Make an offer.

7. Advise unsuccessful applicants.

HIRING STAFF

HIRING STAFF

Before you recruit

1 Write a job description considering future developments.

Check the previous job description and upgrade it if necessary.

List the key tasks and the responsibilities.

- Give the job a realistic title, preferably with some status.
- State why the job is necessary.
- What must be done? Make a list of duties.
- What output do you expect?
- What standard of work do you expect?
- To whom will the person be responsible?
- What staff will they be responsible for?
- List any special work conditions, such as weekend work or shift work.

2 Prepare a person specification.

What sort of person do you need? List the characteristics you require such as traits, skills and abilities. They should include:

- Physical needs - quality of speech, standard of dress, vision, hearing, strength for manual tasks, health etc.

" Don't recruit clones. Build a balanced team."

- Personality required. Do you want a potential leader? Someone good with clients? A problem-solver?
- Experience needed to do the job.
- Educational attainments required. Technical skills, such as computer skills.

Select without bias. Take care not to exclude people on the grounds of sex, race, religion, age, colour, marital status or political beliefs. Your aim is to look for a superior performer best suited to the job to help your organisation reach its goals. But make sure the appointee will fit into the team.

HIRING STAFF

3 Advertise to find suitable applicants.

Consider the environment where your applicant might be found. Where will you advertise? Will you advertise in city newspapers, in trade or professional journals, in colleges, overseas, or will you use an employment agency?

Your advertisement should contain accurate information about the job, the rewards and the competencies required. The more precise you can be with your requirements the less time you will waste sifting and sorting candidates.

If you use an employment agency make sure you supply them with an accurate job description and person specification. Make sure the tests they use are relevant to your vacancy. Don't delegate the final interviews. You know the sort of person you want for your team. Don't recruit people who will always agree with management. You want people who think and are prepared to express their ideas.

Check these stages:

- Decide if you should use an employment agency.

- Advertise the vacancy - how, where, when?

- Select candidates for the final interviews.

- Arrange a venue for interviews and book a suitable room.

- Contact the applicants you have short-listed.

- Contact any people you do not want to interview.

- Do you need to test the applicants?

- Are medical tests required?

- Check references and qualifications if necessary.

- Are you going to be the sole selector or is there going to be a panel of people to interview the candidates?

 Remember

You will never see a bad reference.

HIRING STAFF

The interview

1 Preparing for the interview.

Familiarise yourself with both the job and person specifications. Read each candidate's application and résumé. Contact referees to get further information about an applicant's character, if necessary.

Prepare a sample interview form listing the essential information needed and the types of questions you could ask.

Before the interview:

- If there is to be a panel, brief the members and supply them with a job description, person specification, copies of the application forms and spare interview forms.

- Make sure the interview room is quiet and there are no interruptions.

- When scheduling interviews, allow plenty of time between appointments to make notes and to discuss the candidate.

- Organise a comfortable waiting room.

2 Interview candidates.

Some suggestions for satisfactory interviews:

- Redirect all phone calls and switch off cell phones and pagers.

- Hang an 'Interviews in progress' notice on the door.

- Go to the waiting room and greet the applicants before introducing them to the panel.

- Put them at ease by engaging them in small talk before the serious interview starts.

- Describe the job and clarify any misunderstanding about duties and responsibilities.

- Ask simple open-ended questions.

- Watch their body language and look at their eyes to see how enthusiastic they are about the job.

- Take brief notes.

- Encourage the candidate to ask questions.

- Tell the applicant when a decision will be made.

- Never leave a candidate feeling demoralised. Even if they are unsuitable, finish with a word of praise and a friendly farewell.

- Rate the applicant immediately after the interview.

- Discuss their suitability with other members of the interviewing panel.

3 Decide on the best candidate. Make an offer.

Contact the successful person as soon as possible to make sure they have not accepted another position. Offer the position verbally then put details in writing. Be prepared to negotiate if necessary.

Select a second and a third choice just in case your favoured candidate turns down your offer.

4 Advise unsuccessful applicants.

As soon as possible write to the unsuccessful candidates, advise them of your decision and thank them for applying. Always leave these people feeling they would like to work for you one day. Keep a list of their names and addresses and details of the interviews for future reference.

" Look for ambitious people with a sense of purpose - people with a record of achieving."

INNOVATION

Encourage a creative climate

Innovation flourishes in organisations where it is encouraged, appreciated and rewarded. It dies in organisations that are bureaucratic and critical of change and new ideas.

Ways to promote innovation:

Climate — Foster a working climate where creativity can thrive. Invite and reward good ideas.

Creative planning — Develop a compelling vision. Innovation must come from top management. Share that vision and encourage people to suggest and support new goals and objectives to help achieve it.

Remove barriers — Too many restrictions and barriers prevent ideas from circulating and kill useful ideas. Make rules flexible and remove old regulations. Delegate responsibility down to the action levels of the organisation.

Look for new sources of ideas — Ideas can be found inside and outside the organisation. Watch what other people are doing and copy worthwhile ideas.

Most people have good ideas if you ask the right questions and you are prepared to listen to them.

Encouragement — Showing appreciation of good ideas encourages creativity. Public recognition and rewards can stimulate good ideas. (Rewards can take forms other than money.)

Communication — Everyone should be encouraged to express their ideas. Good communication systems are essential to innovation.

Idea Evaluation — Organisations must be able to sift and assess ideas and learn from their failures and successes. Set up systems to process and evaluate all new ideas.

Criticisms — Criticisms must be discouraged as ideas wither under harsh criticism.

" Innovation thrives on encouragement and dies with routine, regulations and bureaucracy."

INTERPRETER ———————————————

Ensure accuracy

Translating is a difficult task, so when you have to speak through an interpreter, be considerate and try to make the job as easy as possible.

Edit your prepared script and remove any jargon, slang and colloquial expressions. Remove words with double or obscure meanings because these could be interpreted wrongly and cause confusion.

If you intend speaking from a prepared text make sure the interpreter receives a copy to study well before the event. If necessary any figures, statistics or technical terms can be explained and translated before the presentation.

Spend time with your interpreter before your presentation so you can establish a rapport and the interpreter can become familiar with your voice tone and your speaking style.

- Speak slowly and clearly.

- Use simple language. Preferably use words with only one meaning. Use standard English and internationally accepted terms at all times.

- Avoid slang and jargon. Be prepared to explain technical terms.

- Speak in short sentences and short clusters of words.

- Alternate short sections of your presentation with the interpretation. Make your breaks for translation at the end of a thought or a topic.

" Choose your words carefully - to express, not to impress."

- Many people become nervous in front of a large, foreign audience. Take care not to speak too quickly.

- When answering questions, take time to think, answer slowly and use words familiar to the interpreter. (If you lose your train of thought when answering questions, do not worry. Start off in a new direction.)

- When working through an interpreter allow at least double the time taken for a normal talk. Some interpreters feel they should explain things in great detail during a translation and seem to talk for long periods. Be prepared for this and be patient!

INTERVIEWS
When applying for a job

Do your homework thoroughly.

Find out about the organisation you are hoping to join. Annual reports are a good starting point. Talk to staff. Make an appointment and find out what they do — staff trainers and employment officers can be helpful. Ask for a copy of the job description and work out your responses, if asked how you would cope with the jobs on the list.

Dress suitably — the way they would want you to be dressed if you were working for them. Don't wear dark glasses — interviewers like to see your eyes.

Be punctual. Arrive early so you can relax and be composed for the interview. Often a walk before the interview helps you relax.

Take references, curriculum vitae and certificates in case they are needed, but don't flaunt them.

Be polite. Wait until you are asked to sit. Sit up straight — no smoking or chewing gum. Smile, and be natural — don't put on an act.

" You only get one chance to make a first impression!"

If you are asked, be prepared to say why you would like the job and what you hope to contribute. Be modest and honest.

Show you are enthusiastic and keen to get the job.

If you do not understand a question say so. If you cannot answer a question say how you would find the answer. If you cannot do a task say you are willing to learn.

Don't take over the interview. Let the interviewers ask the questions. Try to answer concisely and be prepared to amplify if asked. Don't talk too much.

Your job is to sell yourself. Be friendly, be natural, be enthusiastic, be ambitious about your work and outside interests. Show you are an interesting person and an achiever.

JOB SATISFACTION ————————————

Enjoy your work

Think of the times when you have enjoyed your work. Think of the times when you have been frustrated. This makes a good starting point to consider Herzberg's two-factor theory of job satisfaction.

Satisfiers:

Achievement. You have done a good job to your satisfaction and feel you are making a worthwhile contribution.

Recognition. You are praised and recognised for having done a good job.

Responsibility. You are given responsibility.

Work itself. You enjoy your work and you are given interesting, challenging and creative tasks. You feel you are part of a team.

Growth and advancement. You are advancing in your career and learning new skills.

Dissatisfiers:

Working conditions. Your accommodation, equipment or facilities are unsatisfactory.

Policies and administrative practices. You are subjected to inhibiting rules and frustrating regulations.

Supervision. You are frustrated by excess supervision.

Interpersonal relations. You are working with people you are uncomfortable with.

Salary. You are unhappy with the rewards for your labour.

Status. You are not given the respect you believe you are entitled to.

Job security. You cannot make long term commitments through lack of job security.

Personal life. Your work interferes with your family and your personal life.

" Satisfaction comes from the appreciation and praise for a job well done."

LEADERSHIP

Develop the skills

Leaders are able to influence, guide and shape the attitudes, expectations and behaviour of others. Leaders are not born; they develop. You can become a better leader by studying, practising and acting on constructive feedback from your colleagues.

Here are some suggestions to help you develop as a leader:

Make the most of every opportunity that comes your way. Accept responsibility at work and in professional and social organisations. Volunteer for tasks. Be prepared to work hard for long periods when called upon.

Develop an enthusiastic loyalty to your employer and organisations you support. Take a pride in belonging and offer constructive suggestions for improvements.

Be prepared to work with little or no supervision — make decisions and use your initiative.

Set high standards. Leaders can be recognised because their staff produce superior work and have a higher output.

" Leaders must be prepared to make hard decisions."

Be ambitious. Stretch yourself by setting goals and objectives and work to achieve them.

Learn the skills of people management. Take time to listen to people's complaints, ideas and suggestions. Try counselling and helping staff with personal as well as work-related problems. Delegate work and praise good work — give credit when credit is due.

Develop team leadership skills by improving your communication and training skills.

Attend seminars and training classes and read widely.

Develop your social skills. Make an effort to mix easily with different classes and races of people. Study different cultures and religions. Learn to ask open-ended questions and to develop your listening skills. Dress suitably for occasions. Copy peer dress habits — you will feel more comfortable and will be more likely to be accepted.

Keep calm in times of stress. Avoid producing stress in others and try seeking their help to remove causes of stress. Good communications should help to remove causes of stress.

Make an effort to be flexible. Try adjusting your behaviour to meet the experience, knowledge and skills of others in every situation.

Inspire people to achieve. Expect results.

Focus attention on the important issues.

Delegate, giving clear directions and guidelines. Trust staff and don't interfere.

Accept people as they are. Approach problems and relationships as they are at present not as they were in the past.

 Remember

Do unto others what you would like them to do unto you.

LEADERSHIP

Become a good leader

If you want to be a successful team leader in your organisation you must be prepared to:

1 Accept responsibility.

2 Set high standards.

3 Continuously improve your skills.

4 Develop your social skills.

5 Keep calm in times of stress.

6 Inspire people to achieve.

7 Make time by delegating.

8 Make powerful friends by networking.

9 Have a clear vision.

" Leaders must set high standards and inspire people to achieve."

Are you prepared to work hard at improving your skills?

LEADERSHIP

Aim for these qualities

There are certain qualities of leadership which are accepted universally.

A good leader has the ability to:

1   Build a vision and be focused on that vision.

2   Communicate that vision to all workers.

3   Make quick decisions logically.

4   Be an achiever and get things done by achieving goals.

5   Take risks.

6   Earn respect from workers and clients.

7   Build strong teams.

8   Achieve accountability in the workplace.

LEADERSHIP

Have you these qualities?

*" Leaders must
belong before
they can lead."*

LEADERSHIP

LEADERSHIP

Learn the skills

The traditional models of leadership are breaking down as responsibilities are delegated downwards. As technology delivers information at an ever increasing pace, good leaders are those who can absorb information quickly and use it to make decisions.

The skills of leadership are:

1   To be globally and culturally aware of trends and developments.

2   To be a generalist.

3   To delegate.

4   To embrace change.

5   To be open to diversity.

6   To be a skill builder, a trainer, a coach and a mentor.

7   To be creative.

8   To be a futurist — looking forward at all times.

9   To motivate others.

10 To have a sense of fun.

" Leaders need a clear vision. They should know where they are going."

Have you these skills?

LECTURES

Improve your next lecture

About eighty percent of a presentation is preparation. Try to focus on a simple clear message. A speech is like a journey — it has purpose, direction and an ultimate goal.

Here are three reminder checklists to help you prepare for your next presentation:

1   Preparing a lecture

2   Delivering a lecture

3   Getting more from a lecture

Preparing a lecture

Check these things before you write your lecture:

Your audience

Who are they?

How many are expected?

What are their worries, concerns and interests?

(See also 'Audience Analysis', page 15.)

Your expectations

How much time will you have to speak?

Will there be questions?

Do you need to prepare a handout?

Will reporters be present?

Environment

Where will you be speaking? When?

Are there other speakers? (If so, what are they talking about?)

What other business is on the agenda?

Is there a lectern if you need one?

Will you need a microphone?

Are there facilities for visual aids?

" *When preparing a speech keep in mind the fleeting nature of oral communication.*"

Your topic is... (Write it out.)

Do you want to:

Introduce a speaker

Thank a speaker

Support a proposal

Inform or instruct your audience

Convince people

Inspire or motivate your audience

Get action on a proposal

Entertain your audience?

Decide exactly what you want to do.

Aim (Objective)

Your aim is to ...

What responses do you really want?

Lecture outline

What is your main message? (Write it down very briefly.)

Then organise your most important points and supporting statements by clustering or mind mapping.

1 Your first main point leading to...

2 Second point, leading to...

3 Third point etc.

Conclusion

Summarise your main points

Give a memorable message

Call for action, if appropriate. (Appeals must be realistic.)

Now go back and rewrite your introduction.

Your introduction should:

Get attention

Arouse interest

Reveal the purpose of the talk

Establish a rapport with your audience

Next decide on the title

Make it interesting, intriguing and appealing. (Add an explicit sub-title if necessary.)

Visual aids

What visual aids do you need to reinforce the message?

They must be simple, understood and seen by all!

Some of the most effective tools you should use are:

The real thing

Demonstrations

Movie projector

Video

Models

Overhead projector

Slide projector

Handouts

Warnings

1. **Spoken language is different from written language.**

    Rewrite articles or reports in the spoken language.

2. **Lectures should never be read. After you have written out the spoken version pick out key memory words and speak to them.**

LECTURES

LECTURES

Deliver them confidently

Helpful hints

Dress for your audience. Your clothes should be comfortable and suit the occasion.

Before you are due to speak get the 'feel' of the room and the audience. Sit at the back of the room and observe other speakers and the reactions of the audience.

During a break check the sound system to get your levels right and to see how you adjust the microphone height.

When you get up to speak take time to compose yourself. Adjust the lectern, arrange your notes, adjust the microphone, take a deep breath, look the audience over, smile at a friend and when you are ready, start.

Always address the Chair. The preferred forms of address are 'Mister Chairman' or 'Madam Chair'.

The way you begin is very important. That's when you establish your credentials and build a rapport with your audience.

Don't read; talk to your audience. Use key words as memory joggers.

" The end should be a climax, not an anti-climax."

Share your feelings. Talk about your experiences and emotions. Be enthusiastic about your subject.

Watch your audience. Can they all hear you? If they look bored tell them a story. If they look weary give them a break.

If you 'dry up' don't panic. Ask for questions or pause and compose yourself — make it look a natural break. Then start off on another point.

Use good visual aids — they can save you a lot of explaining. But they must be simple and be able to be seen by all.

Your conclusion is very important. It is the last chance you will have to leave a memorable message. Spend time fully preparing a strong conclusion.

LECTURES

Get more from them

If you are a member of the audience, you can learn more from a lecture if you follow a few simple rules.

Before the lecture
Read as much as you can about the topic.
Select your seat carefully
Choose a comfortable seat, away from distractions. Make sure you will be able to hear the speaker clearly and see all the visual aids.

Give your undivided attention to the speaker
Concentrate on what the speaker is saying. Watch for body language. Listen for areas of particular interest. Listen for new information. Ask yourself, "What's in this for me?"

Make brief notes using your own form of shorthand
Jot down headings to increase your recall.

Look for 'facts' and 'principles'. Don't write down details or you will miss important points.

Keep an open mind
Don't stop listening because of your preconceived ideas or your biases. 'Emotional blackouts' make you lose the thread of the talk.

Don't create distractions
Don't talk to people sitting near you or try to make clever remarks. Don't read or doodle — look at the speaker.

Keep asking yourself questions
Use the five 'W's and two 'H's — Who, what, why, when, where, how and how much.

Keep summarising and reviewing
Weigh up the evidence as it is presented.

Ask the speaker questions.
Don't be afraid to ask if you do not understand something or if you want further information.

LECTURES

" If you ask a question you may look foolish for five minutes, but if you don't you remain a fool for ever."

 Remember

People who make brief notes remember more.

LETTERS

Keep to the point

You can influence and motivate people with a well written letter. Business letters should be well set out and free from error. They should have:

> An opening paragraph. Quote references or mention previous correspondence.
>
> The main message. Be brief and factual.
>
> A polite closure. Finish with a direct statement telling the reader what action you require. Offer further help.

Rules for good business writing:

1   Answer letters, faxes and e-mail promptly.

2   Highlight points to be answered and jot notes in the margin of the letter.

3   Assemble relevant material necessary for drafting your response.

4   Prepare a draft letter setting out references, addresses, names and dates in logical order.

5   Keep your message brief.

6   Get to the point quickly.

7   Use plain language.

8   Keep sentences and paragraphs short.

9   Be firm, positive and helpful.

10 Revise your draft.

11 Set out the letter neatly. Good layout is essential.

12 Proofread the letter carefully. Remove all surplus words and check your spelling and punctuation.

13 Use good quality paper and envelopes.

" The important thing is to tell people what they want to know, not what you want to tell them."

Letters to collect debts

The collection process goes through distinct stages. The first and second letters can be used as reminders. It's diplomatic to assume the customer has overlooked payment and will pay when reminded. The third letter can take the form of an inquiry. You can ask for an explanation of the circumstances that prevent payment. If there is no satisfactory explanation, a fourth letter should demand urgent action.

1   The reminder

Assume the customer has overlooked the bill.

" This is a friendly reminder that your account is overdue. Perhaps you have mailed your cheque already. If so thank you."

2   Strong reminder

Assume the customer has overlooked paying. Reassure the customer that credit is still available.

" Most of our customers appreciate a reminder when their account is overdue. You may have already mailed payment. If so, thank you. If not, will you please do so at your earliest convenience. We look forward to being of service to you in the future."

3   Inquiry or explanation stage

By this time you assume there is a reason why the customer has not paid. Try appealing to the customer's pride by avoiding the embarrassment of a bad credit record. Appeal to their self-interest by reminding them of the value of credit. If you receive a satisfactory explanation there is a good chance payment will eventually be made.

" Try to maintain goodwill even if the debt is overdue."

" Please contact us immediately if you find you are unable to pay. Together we should be able to work something out."

4   Urgency or final stage

Impress on the customer the seriousness of the situation. Point out what the customer has to lose if the bill is not paid. Be demanding and imply the possibility of legal action.

"Please send your cheque immediately, or contact us so a payment plan can be arranged. If you act now your valuable credit rating will be maintained."

Letters to deal with complaints

Letters dealing with complaints should be polite and helpful and end on a friendly note.

The opening paragraph

The opening paragraph should identify the problem or request and show that you agree in principle with the person's right to complain or request something.

"Thank you for bringing the problem to our notice. It is only by such actions we can improve our service to our clients."

The message

State what you are going to do about the problem, i.e. refuse, replace or refund.

1   Give reasons

If your refusal is based on good reasons, state these clearly. Take the reader in to your confidence. Do not talk down to clients.

"We have sold five thousand of these units last year without one single complaint."

2   Give a clear refusal

The refusal should follow logically from the reason given.

"We are not prepared to refund your money because you have had six months' use of the unit and we suspect the servicing by an unauthorised electrician has been at fault."

" *If you respect your client and handle a complaint fairly your business will grow.* "

The closure

End on a positive note showing a concern for your client.

"If you could bring the unit in to our workshop we will overhaul it and charge you only for replacement parts. We hope we can solve this problem to our mutual satisfaction."

Letters to the editor

To publicise your ideas try writing letters to the editors of prestigious newspapers.

Here are some guidelines:

State your ideas or complaint clearly at the beginning of your letter.

Don't be offensive. You will get more impact with restrained language than with abuse.

Use humour and satire.

Avoid topics such as religion and racial controversy, blasphemy and issues which could be libellous.

Start with an attention-grabbing introduction and your strongest argument. Arrange your statements in logical order. Leave your weaker arguments to near the end because that is the part that will be left out if the letter is too long, or space is not available.

Keep your sentences and paragraphs short.

When you have drafted your letter remove all jargon, clichés and unnecessary words.

The shorter your letter, the better the chance of it being published.

" Humour and satire hit where it hurts most."

Letters to the editor

Letters to sell

Before you write a sales letter, learn as much as you can about your product.

What can it do?

What are its main features?

How does it differ from its competitors?

How much will it sell for?

What materials is it made from?

...and so on.

Next research the market.

Analyse potential customers.

Where do they live?

What is their average income?

Get the reaction of a representative sample of the group to your product.

Sales letter strategy

1   Catch the reader's attention

"Cut your electricity bills in half."

" Sell benefits not products."

2   Stimulate the reader's interest

"Our new energy /solar water heaters have a revolutionary design. They will burn waste materials, such as your junk mail and plastic bags, and they use solar energy. They have no working parts to go wrong."

3   Develop a desire for your product

Aim for the response, *"I would like to have one of those."*

"Just think what you could do with the extra money. It's like a pay rise!"

4   Encourage action

"If you mail the enclosed card today, our representative will telephone and make an appointment to call. We will discuss your needs and give you a free quotation. You are under no obligation to buy."

LISTENING

Be patient and encouraging

You cannot listen if you are doing all the talking — and if you are not listening you are not learning. So for better listening, stop talking, concentrate on what the other person wants to tell you.

Remove distractions

For an important interview look for a quiet room without distractions.

Put the other person at ease

Start with friendly, everyday comfortable conversation to establish a rapport.

Encourage the speaker by putting their feelings into words. If they are upset over a decision, or worried about a problem, try:

" *I am sorry to hear my decision has upset you. I appreciate what you are telling me. Tell me what we can do about the problem?"*

Show that you want to listen

Look and act as if you are interested. Give the speaker your full attention. Show you are listening by nodding and making encouraging remarks. *"Yes, I see what you mean."*

Empathise with the speaker

Try to put yourself in the speaker's shoes to see their point of view. Ask yourself: *"Why did they say that? What would I have said?"*

Be patient

Allow plenty of time for listening when you make appointments. Don't interrupt. Don't keep looking at your watch.

" A wise man talks little, an ignorant one talks much."

Control your emotions

If you get emotional you will not hear properly. You will get the wrong meanings from words and you could get the wrong message.

Avoid argument and criticism

Ask questions to draw the speaker out. *"Why did you say that? Is that what you really feel? What facts have you to support that statement?"*

Don't argue or attack. If you put speakers on the defensive they may become withdrawn or get emotional.

Ask questions

Questions encourage the speaker and show you were listening. Ask questions for amplification. It helps to develop a topic. Ask : *"Why do you believe that?"*

Summarise, review and reflect

From time to time summarise what you think the speaker has said and repeat the speaker's words. This will help the speaker and help you remember.

MANAGING

Plan for success

1 Recruit the best

Recruit the best people you can find. Use structured interviews and if you are interviewing candidates for senior positions, psychological and aptitude tests are helpful. Look for weaknesses in an applicant's character or qualifications.   Ask them about any achievements they are particularly proud of. This will give you an idea of their aspirations and hopes and whether they will be an asset in your organisation.

2 Set standards

Make sure your staff understand clearly what you expect from them. Explain your vision and the values you respect and want to see upheld.

Staff should have an outward focus. They should know the changing needs of customers and clients. This means new products, new horizons and enhanced communication technology. You must come up with a new product or enhanced services every two or three years to survive. Change must become the norm for all dynamic organisations.

3 Involve staff and clients in planning

Get your clients and customers involved in new developments and in helping to design the restructuring of the organisation.

" Learn to manage yourself, then you are qualified to manage others"

Everyone has clients.

All staff must know who their clients are, what they want, and what they expect.

Planning should be carried out with staff and customers. It should begin with a wide survey to examine the environmental climate the teams will work in. Study the current political, economic, technical, internal and social environments to identify changes which could affect the organisation, or for which there needs to be a response. Then teams and individuals should set their goals for change.

4   Teams must meet formally to review progress

Call regular meetings to review team progress and to share ideas, and monthly meetings to change plans where necessary. These meetings must be well planned and involve all participants.

A plan is not a static thing — it's dynamic and changes must be made to respond to a changing environment. Good ideas just don't happen once a year! A good manager is constantly making environmental scans and identifying outside changes. *"What's happening out there?" "Who is doing a better job than us, and why is it better?" "What can we do better?"*

5   Walk about and listen to staff and clients

Don't spend all your time behind your desk. Keep your door open to staff and customers. Network, travel and look!

6   Act like a manager

Be enthusiastic and talk about your vision for the future. Become a mentor, a coach a trainer. Be positive, diplomatic and sympathetic.

7   Respond to a crisis fast

Troubles must be fixed quickly. Keep staff informed of developing situations. Make fast decisions. Learn to make balanced judgements.

8   Respond to all messages rapidly

Try to respond to all messages within 24 hours if possible.

9   Be honest, fair, consistent, insistent and persistent!

10 Never compromise deeply held principles.

MANAGING

Anticipate future trends

The electronic revolution has changed the world we live in. Tomorrow's managers must change with it if their organisations are to survive.

Here are some of the characteristics of the new workplace that tomorrow's managers and leaders will need to know about and to understand:

How to bring about constant change in organisations without upsetting staff and clients.

The effect of 'flatter' organisations with fewer middle managers and changes in traditional organisational structures.

The need for flexible work locations and more effective and efficient work practices.

The impact of less direct supervision; the effect of more trust and more accountability.

Greater work decentralisation and flexible working days and hour options.

The need to integrate work and family life and help people achieve this.

There will be a large growth in temporary employees.

The impact of less stable and part-time work forces.

How to handle part-time and contract workers.

Individuals will need a greater range of skills and greater flexibility.

The major impact of electronic information systems.

How to experiment and keep up with this rapidly changing technology.

How to set up, run, coordinate and mentor work teams.

The importance of coaching, training and mentoring.

How to turn businesses into heavily customer-orientated organisations.

How to establish alliances and networks for mutual benefits.

" Nothing endures except change."

 Remember

There is difficulty in getting messages out to clients and new customers because of the increasing competition for people's time from other organisations and the media.

MANAGING

Qualities most admired

Think about managers and team leaders you have known or worked for and make a list of the qualities you most admire in employers.

The following list was compiled by participants from South East Asian management workshops. Common comments were:

"I like my boss. He listens to me and involves me in decision making".
"Good managers have the ability to discover the ability in others."

A good manager:

Has a strategic vision.

Achieves goals.

Can delegate authority.

Is organised.

Can make tough decisions.

Makes decisions objectively.

Does not procrastinate.

Has no favourites.

Is enthusiastic about work.

Has an unquenchable curiosity.

Maintains a positive attitude.

Delivers on promises.

Is committed to team work.

Can give honest feedback.

Treats all staff the same.

Is prepared to consider new ideas.

Asks relevant questions.

Is an active listener.

Keeps staff fully informed of developing situations.

" Good managers have humanity, humility and humour and the courage to make unpopular decisions for the good of the organisation and the staff."

Can persuade and influence.

Expresses feelings honestly.

Knows each employee by name.

Takes an interest in them.

Shows confidence in subordinates.

Gives credit where credit is due.

Looks at the broader issues.

Does not argue over petty matters.

Gives employees incentives to improve.

Raises issues and problems early.

Acknowledges own mistakes and shortcomings.

MEDIA INTERVIEWS

Seek publicity

If you want publicity for a cause, or you want to refute a misunderstanding, prepare your story well before contacting a journalist.

1 Define your purpose

The more specifically you can state your purpose the more successful will be the interview. Both parties need to agree on the purpose at the beginning of the interview.

2 Clarify your thoughts

Why do you want to be interviewed?

Write down the reason that your story is newsworthy.

Are you giving your opinion on a topical issue?

Are you trying to clarify a position or eliminate a misunderstanding?

Do you want to inform on people responsible for undesirable activities?

Are you seeking publicity for a cause?

Do you want free advertising for an event, product or service?

3 Assemble all the facts

Provide the journalist with background information well before the interview.

The more notes, references and clippings you can supply the better.

4 Preliminary planning

Write down the topics that you would like to cover in the interview. Plan your strategy and study all the details. You will then be in a better position to cope with any deviations and to help bring the interview back on to the part of the topic you want to discuss.

5 Meeting the journalist

The first impressions you make are important and may determine how the entire interview proceeds. Be friendly and polite, allow time for small talk and time to relax.

6 Getting down to business

Be yourself, share your emotions and feelings, be honest but diplomatic. Don't make wild statements you cannot substantiate.

Even if things are a little tense at first they usually settle down as the interview proceeds. The more evasive or nervous you become the more the journalist will probe.

Try to illustrate your replies using anecdotes - they always make an interview more interesting.

7 Threatening questions

Most interviewers will ask some questions you would rather avoid. Prepare for these questions just in case you are asked. Make a list of such topics and draft possible replies during your planning stage.

8 Take care at the finish

When asked if you have any *'final thoughts'* use this time to briefly summarise your main message. Be confident and sincere and aim for a strong conclusion.

After the interview when you are relaxing take care not to make an informal comment, observation or criticism.

" It's what people want to know that's important - not what you want to tell them!"

MEDIA SUPPORT

MEDIA SUPPORT

Work for mutual benefits

Sooner or later you will need the support of the media to get your ideas and messages to your target audience. To get this you must understand the role of the media and the needs of reporters. Both the print and the broadcast media are in the business of making money and meeting deadlines.

If you want publicity for your cause or your business you will need to take the initiative. It is your job to make contact with reporters if you have a message to get across. Make sure your message is news, not propaganda or free advertising.

Foster good relations

Get to know the reporters in your area. Make an effort to establish a good working relationship. Be honest with them and work to build up a mutual trust.

Good media relations take time and effort but they pay dividends.

Give reporters leads for stories. Prepare your material well for them. Give them good briefings and supply accurate information.

" A controversy with the press, in the press, is the controversy of a fly with a spider."
Sir Henry Taylor

Often misreporting occurs because people do not take time to explain what they really mean — they take things for granted.

If you are misquoted contact the reporter first and try to discuss the problem in a friendly manner. If you storm into the editor's office to complain you will lose the reporter's respect and friendship.

Helping reporters

Give as much advance notice as possible of coming events. Follow up with reminder calls.

Supply copy if possible. Make your messages as clear and concise as possible and enclose background material.

Type your message on one side of the paper using half sheets.

Double space the typing leaving wide margins.

Leave a large space at the top of the first page.

Put your name and telephone number on the top of the first page.

Number the pages clearly.

Never break a paragraph going from one page to the next.

Be cooperative

If reporters want a story, try to help — you may need their help one day.

Try to give accurate, factual information.

If you do not have the information, suggest where it might be found, or offer to get it.

If you say you will call back at a certain time, keep your word. Remember, journalists have strict deadlines to meet.

Coverage of events

Send advance detailed information as soon as possible to the editor.

Keep following up with newsworthy, human interest stories as they develop. The names and achievements of distinguished guests can make interesting reading and publicise your event.

On the day of the event make life easy for reporters. Arrange for them to have a table and a light near the speaker. Supply them with a programme and copy of the speakers' papers. Arrange for someone to act as their host and give them any help they require.

Often they need a quiet room for typing up copy.

Hints from experienced journalists

Hard facts stop speculation. You can kill criticism and stop rumours with a timely, honest, factual story.

Never say "No comment" unless you want a full investigation carried out.

When you come out of a meeting be prepared to answer tricky questions. Being unprepared is a sure way to a bad press.

Don't be upset if a reporter uses a tape recorder — it helps to get your story right.

MEETINGS

MEETINGS

Keep to the agenda

An agenda lists the items to be dealt with at a meeting. It helps the chairperson keep the meeting to a sequence, control the time and accomplish the business more efficiently and effectively.

If you are the chairperson, draw up your own agenda. Never let others do it for you.

A suggested agenda:

1   Open the meeting

2   Apologies

3   Welcome new members and guests

4   Minutes of previous meeting

5   Business arising from the minutes

6   Correspondence

7   Business arising from correspondence

8   Financial report

" A good agenda keeps meetings on track and saves hours."

9   General business of which notice has been given

10   Reports from committees

11   Business arising from reports

12   Other general business — with consent of the meeting

13   Notices of motion for future meetings

14   Announce date and time of next meeting

15   Close the meeting

MEETINGS

Be an efficient chairperson

If you fail to prepare for your next meeting, then prepare to fail.

Before the meeting, the chairperson should:

Be familiar with the constitution or bylaws.

Know the minimum number (quorum) that must be present to conduct business.

Know the correct voting procedures and whether notices of motions need to be given prior to the meeting (and if so, how many days before).

Prepare the meeting agenda with the secretary.

Make sure the secretary has given due notice of the meeting to all members.

Read the minutes of the previous meeting to see what business needs following up.

At the meeting:

Start (and finish) on time.

See whether a quorum is present.

Call the meeting to order — formally.

Keep to the agenda.

Keep speakers within the rules of the meeting procedures.

Preserve order and courtesy.

Remain neutral during debates.

Keep a sense of humour. Keep calm. Do not dominate.

Call speakers in the correct sequence after they have indicated they wish to speak.

Decide on points of order.

Prevent irrelevant and repetitious discussions.

You may appoint committees and exercise a casting vote.

You should not refuse motions if they have a seconder.

" The chairperson's role is to protect the weak, to control the strong, and make the best use of the talent present."

You may rule for or against the following motions....

"That the question not now be put."

"That the matter be referred to a committee."

"That the debate be adjourned."

"That the meeting now adjourn."

"That the Chair's ruling be dissented from."

"That the meeting no longer has confidence in the Chair."

At the finish:

Summarise and reach conclusions.
After the meeting follow up and coordinate to see that things get done.

MEETINGS

MEETINGS

Run better meetings

Meetings have an unfortunate reputation because many are time-wasters. They often last too long, are ineffective because of unclear objectives and are poorly run. Your reputation can depend on how well you run a meeting.

Call a meeting only when it is necessary.

Plan and prepare yourself for all meetings.

Have clear and achievable objectives.

Prepare and distribute an agenda.

Keep to starting and finishing times.

Keep control. Stop people digressing. Know the rules, give clear directions, listen carefully, summarise often and keep on schedule.

Get things done. Action by whom? By when?

Make the most of the talent and experience present.

Review and summarise often.

Record recommendations and give members responsibilities for specific tasks.

Evaluate meetings. Can we do better next time?

" Keep looking for ways to improve on your last meeting."

Tips

Make your meetings interesting by adding variety and humour. Invite visitors to speak. Break your meeting up with surprise events. Pause for a brief brainstorming session from time to time. Try problem-solving sessions. Make presentations and use visual aids. Give demonstrations.

If things start to drag, stop for a coffee break or adjourn the meeting.

Allow time for a meeting to 'warm up' before important items are introduced.

Save interesting items for the time when your meeting starts to drag.

Don't bring up important items when people are tired.

Good news should be saved until the end to finish the meeting on a high note.

MEMO or MEMORANDUM

Request action

Ideally, a memo follows a discussion and an agreement on what has to be done in a project. It is a written instruction on what actions are needed and who should do specific tasks.

If written simply and concisely, it conveys a sense of urgency. Each member of a team should learn exactly how their job fits into the project and what they have to do.

The rules for writing a memo are simple:

- The main message comes first. Start with the action you want taken.

- Talk your ideas through to yourself before you write. Write the way you talk. Pretend you are talking to one person.

- Be brief and to the point using simple language and short sentences.

- Put your ideas in a logical order.

- Try to keep all memos to one page or less.

- Use a simple easy-to-read layout.

- Use clear headings.

- Proofread carefully. Check your language, your spelling and grammar. Avoid jargon and gobbledegook.

- When sending copies, list names in alphabetical order of surnames. This could be more acceptable than listing in order of rank because it avoids personal jealousies.

" Choose your words carefully - to express, not to impress."

MONEY

Invest soundly

Most people save for a purpose. It could be to buy a house, a car or a business but usually it is for a secure retirement. With increased life expectancy, your retirement could cover 25 or 30 years – a third of your lifetime.

Here are some guidelines for investing your hard-earned money.

- **Spend less than you earn.** Save regularly. Try to save at least 10 percent of your salary each pay-day. Don't be someone who spends first and then tries to save what is left. If possible arrange an automatic deduction each pay-day and budget from what remains.

- **Save early.** The length of time you invest increases the amount of money you receive by an impressive amount. Learn the power of compounding interest to boost your returns so the sooner you start the greater your returns.

- **Give priority to paying off any high interest debts.** This is very important during times of low inflation. **Pay off credit card loans as soon as possible!**

- **Budget to live within your means.** Jot down all your expenses for two months to see how you spend your money. Decide what is essential and what is not essential. Reduce your non-essential spending.

- **Set investment goals.** Plan what you want, by when. Focus on diversified assets, and assets that can be easily converted into cash during an emergency.

- **Become knowledgeable about investing before you start.** Read books about investing and learn to study investment statements. Seek objective, independent, professional advice. Do your homework and you will save money and reduce your stress.

- **Spread your risks**. Spread your money over several different types of investments such as bonds, shares, property, and income-based assets.

" The more you sow, the more you reap."

MONEY

- **Develop a strategy**. If you have plenty of time, you can invest conservatively for the long term. You may have to take greater risks if you are investing for a short time. Consider using professional financial advisers as they have access to more information and advice from research teams. Managed funds reduce share risks by making a wider spread of investments.

 Remember

Don't put all your eggs in one basket.

" Money is a good servant but a bad master!"

- **Consider an employer-subsidised superannuation scheme.**

MOTIVATION

Stimulate workers

Even if people are fairly treated and have pleasant working conditions, they do not do their best work until they have the freedom to show what they are capable of doing and are motivated to do it.

What motivates people?

1   More responsibility

2   Pride in doing a good job

3   Personal growth and development

4   Advancement and recognition of achievement.

1   More responsibility

If you delegate authority you are telling your people you trust them. Most people will respond to the challenge and be motivated to make a special effort to succeed.

2   Pride in doing a good job

We have a great feeling of satisfaction when we have done our best and we can show off our skills. We are proud when others know we have done a good job.

Tell your staff when they have done a good job — praise loudly!

" You get loyalty and commitment from people by giving it to them."

3   Personal growth and development

Make work more interesting by giving people more opportunities to try different tasks and to show what they can do. Encourage workers to study, attend training sessions and seminars, join clubs and educational groups and travel.

4   Advancement and recognition of achievement

Sincere praise and simple rewards for good work will usually stimulate workers to increase their efforts and this could lead to advancement in the organisation.

MOTIVATION

Reactivate your people

Many employees get bored with their job; they become discontented and their productivity declines. When this happens try to counsel them and challenge them with new tasks.

1   Discuss the problem with the employee.

    Express your concerns and ask them about their life goals and objectives. What do they want from work? Explain you want to help them.

2   Try to isolate areas of concern. Often lack of feedback for a job well done turns people off their work and makes them cynical about the organisation.

3   Suggest new challenges and seek their reaction and views. Offer to arrange training them for new tasks. Give them special assignments or suggest job rotation.

4   Ask for their ideas on ways to improve their job and their work output.

5   Rewrite their job specifications and their work contract.

6   Stimulate them by suggesting new career prospects.

    "We plan to open a new branch next year. If we train you for the position would you be interested in moving to take up the position of manager?"

7   Be prepared to listen to their personal troubles. Counsel them if you can, or arrange for a professional counsellor to help them.

8   When they have reached their highest level in your organisation with little further career prospects, retrain them for another department or find them another job.

9   Encourage them to join outside organisations and they may be stimulated to learn new skills. Their confidence could be increased and they could have a new status to maintain e.g. the president of a local Rotary club or a sports club.

10 Reassure the employee you are interested in their ideas and their work and you plan to follow their progress on a regular basis.

" People work harder when they are encouraged and there is something in it for them. "

MOTIVATION TIPS

Recognise good work

Spend quality time with your people. Listen to their grievances and show an interest in their work and their achievements. Your interest and concerns will pay dividends.

Remember names

We appreciate it if people remember our names so make an effort to remember names of others.

Try repeating them, make notes of names, try to associate names with faces, or with other people, or things, or places.

Involve staff in decision making

Encourage ideas on how jobs can be done better, how working conditions can be improved and how quality standards can be raised.

Be honest with your people

Keep them informed of any problems or difficulties. Share your vision with them. Share information with them.

Reward your people for effort and ideas

Make people feel like winners. Rewards may take many forms — bonus payments; salary increases; a new position; time off; a car park; a company car; a prize; a paid holiday or some other form of recognition.

" Make people feel like winners."

Praise

Everyone needs praise. Look for things to praise but praise only if it is warranted. Be specific and sincere.

Remove controls

Try removing controls, increasing the amount of responsibility you give your staff and make them accountable for their own work.

Challenging assignments

Give difficult or demanding projects to staff who enjoy a challenge.

NAMES

Remember people's names

Most of us are good at remembering faces but are often embarrassed when we are introducing someone because we have forgotten their name.

People are flattered if you refer to them by name. Many people owe their success to their ability to recall names and details. To help become a successful leader or manager make an effort to master the art of remembering names.

Here are some suggestions to help you improve your recall of people's names:

- After meeting and being introduced to a person for the first time discuss their name with them.

  "Is your name spelt with an 'e' or an 'o' at the end? Are you by any chance related to John Andersen from Picton?"

- The most basic and reliable memory device is a note on a piece of paper. Always carry a small notebook and jot down the new name so you can put it in your diary or in your address book. A notebook can be a sound investment if you travel widely and meet a large number of people or manage a large staff.

- Keep using the name. Repetition is a good memory tool.

- You can often relate the new name to another person with a similar name.

- Often the name has a meaning you can associate with an object, or another person, such as Mr Foot, Mrs Cook or Dr Swan.

- Sometimes you can relate a name to a characteristic of the person - Mrs Smart or Mr Blunt, for example.

Make the effort to master the skill of remembering names.

You must be prepared to work at it, but it is worth the effort. People will be flattered when you greet them by name especially if you haven't seen them for a long time.

" A person's name is the most important sound they can hear."

NEGOTIATION

Concentrate on reaching an agreement

Successful leaders must be skilled negotiators. They must know how to compromise and reach agreements.

Here are some principles to keep in mind next time you negotiate:

1   Try to look at things from the other side's point of view.

2   Look for options where there are mutual gains.

3   Look for problems below the surface — not the obvious problems, the unspoken ones.

4   Try to separate people and personalities from the situation.

5   Always consider the economics of the various solutions.

6   Focus on mutual interests not on non-negotiable positions.

7   To gain something be prepared to give something.

Hints

Do your homework thoroughly and plan a strategy.

Write down what you want to achieve and your final position. Then try to do the same for the other side.

Be polite and ethical and NEVER lose your temper under any circumstances.

Emphasise common concerns and points of agreement.

Seek information by questioning to probe and clarify issues. Use basic language where possible.

Respect confidentiality of talks and asides and express appreciation for the other side's time and efforts. Weigh up and evaluate options. *"These are the consequences if we do this"* and *"This is what will happen if we do that..."*

Keep discussions on track and moving. Write up issues and interests for all to see and think about.

Make a special effort to listen carefully, especially for hidden meanings. Jot down reminder notes.

" If you are patient in one moment of anger, you will escape a hundred days of sorrow."

NEGOTIATION

Overcome deadlocks and stalemates

When further negotiations seem impossible:

Adjourn to rethink and consult.

Review progress, stressing the positive side of negotiations.

Restate common concerns.

Write up issues and developments for all parties to study and think about.

Consider the outcome if negotiations fail.

Say honestly how you feel about the situation.

Ask, "What if we do this... or that?" Be prepared to give something if you want something.

Talk about positive past relationships and how both parties have benefited.

State the long term benefits of an agreement and what the consequences will be if an agreement is not reached. State negative results concisely and clearly.

Move to a different issue to give time to think about the consequences of an impasse.

*" You only fail
when you
give up."*

If everything fails:

Set a date for another meeting and walk out.

OBJECTIVES

Set targets

An objective is like a journey. It must have a purpose, a map (plan), resources (a budget), a direction, a timetable (a schedule) and a destination - and you will need to know when you have arrived. An objective is more specific than a goal because it should define the conditions to be met and the exact target to be achieved by a certain time. Objectives should be **SMART**: **S**pecific, **M**easurable, **A**chievable, **R**ealistic and completed on **T**ime.

For example:

If you are a manager and your goal is to increase the profits to your shareholders over the next year, your objectives could be:

- To investigate and recommend ways to overcome problems of absenteeism and reduce them to less than 3 percent in the next six months.

- To streamline office procedures and reduce the number of office staff to eight by December this year.

- Two months from this date, to identify at least five new suppliers selling cheaper, high quality raw materials for manufacturing our products.

… and so on.

Objectives should be written out in basic language so everyone involved understands what is to be done, who will do the jobs, when they should be finished and how management will know when the results have been achieved.

Tasks to be done

Once you have set the objectives you must plan the operation carefully.

1   Prepare a list of tasks.

2   Plan who will be responsible for specific jobs.

3   State when they should be completed.

4   You will need resources to achieve your objective, so you must plan what staff, money or materials are required. How will these resources be obtained and allocated? Budgeting and allocation of resources will probably be one of your most difficult tasks.

5   Inform all the people involved about the objective and what is expected of them. **It is essential to involve your work team at the planning stage.** They must fully understand and be committed to achieving the desired result by a realistic date.

6   Monitor all activities to make sure they are proceeding according to plan.

7   Inform management about progress at regular intervals.

" At the beginning there was much to do, but by planning and whittling away, the tasks became few."

ORDERS and DIRECTIVES ————————

Be clear

The days of strict orders and directives have gone. These days leaders give directives to teams by requesting or suggesting action and focus on organisational goals rather than on their own objectives.

Make sure your instructions are clear, simple and unambiguous. Use active, specific and familiar words. With verbal instructions ask the employee to repeat the order, so there are no misunderstandings.

With complex instructions write them out first to get your own ideas clear. Give appropriate staff a copy. When they have had a chance to study them, be available to answer any questions and discuss points raised.

Useful guidelines for giving orders and directives:

1 Be clear and definite about what you want done.

2 Give reasons and assign priority to the new task.

3 Set deadlines.

4 State, illustrate or demonstrate the results you expect.

5 Set prescribed standards.

6 Verify that the directive is within the job description or the person's employment contract.

7 Ask questions to ensure understanding and encourage questions.

8 Make the person or team accountable for the task.

9 Respect employee's dignity. Take care not to talk down to them.

" How well we get our message across is determined not by how well we say things, but by how well we are understood."

PERSUASION

Listen for persuasive rhetoric

Be aware of some of the techniques people use to influence you or to persuade you to buy a product. You may be able to turn them to your advantage.

Speakers and advertisers often use the following techniques:

- **Testimonials by famous people**

  Actors, sportspersons, TV presenters or famous people are often used to establish the credibility of a product or an organisation. You should remember they are paid to sell the concept or the product even though they may know little about it.

- **Keeping up with the neighbours**

  This technique relies on peer pressure and changing fashions.

  "Everyone has one; why not you?"

- **"I am successful - despite my humble background."**

  "I can show you how you too can be successful." "You should vote for me. I know all about your problems."

- **Common associations**

  A respected or prestigious organisation or sport is sometimes associated with a product. Unfortunately sport is often associated with liquor or tobacco advertising, so be aware of this connection.

- **Unsupported claims**

  Listen for claims which cannot be supported by proven facts. Don't believe everything just because you hear it many times or because it is printed in large bold letters.

- **Selection of favourable evidence**

  Speakers and advertisers often use half-truths and omit unfavourable evidence. The media often make a story out of 'half-baked' facts. This is called *'card stacking'*. It is a powerful method of persuasion.

- **Exaggerated distinctions**

  Often a unique feature of a product or an idea is highlighted and treated as if it is of great value. It may be of little real value or benefit.

- **Name-calling**

  Sometimes a speaker denounces a person or an idea by associating them with things feared, distrusted or despised. The name-caller wants to discredit the other person. This technique is often used by politicians.

" Listen with a sensitive ear. Hear and try to understand other points of view."

PRAISING

PRAISING

Enhance your relationships

Discover the power of praise — it will make your world a better place.

Praising and saying "Thank you" is a neglected skill. A few words of approval can improve the performance of staff and enhance relationships.

To maximise the benefits of praise, here are a few tips:

1 Praise only if it is warranted.

2 People need praise. Find something to praise in each person.

3 Be sincere.

4 Make eye contact, and thank the person by name.

5 Be specific. Tell people what they did well.

6 Don't praise to cover reprimands.

7 Go public with your praise. If you acknowledge efforts in front of colleagues it is often more meaningful and could inspire others.

" Praise loudly — blame softly."

Praise in public, criticise in private.

PRESENTATIONS

Golden rules for success

1   **Analyse the situation and your audience**

What is the purpose of your presentation.

Who will be in your audience?

What action do you want your audience to take?

What do they know about your subject?

What is important to them?

What do you want them to remember about your presentation?

2   **Do your homework**

Eighty percent of a successful presentation is in the preparation.

Focus on a simple, clear message. People will remember only three or four key points so don't use too many facts and figures.

Plan your presentation so you have a good opening to establish a rapport with your audience.

3   **Catch their attention**

Get your audience's attention right from the start. Use a gimmick or tell a story. Do not lecture them - chat to them.

Audiences remember about 20 percent of what they hear and about 80 percent of what they see so demonstrate and use visuals. Keep your visual aids simple and don't overdo them.

4   **Practice makes perfect**

Make sure you can use your audio-visual equipment confidently. Have a practice in the presentation room so you are familiar with how everything operates and the sources of electric power. Check the room's blackout facilities and the position of the light switches as well as how to work the heating and air conditioning units.

5   **Get your message across**

Tell them what you are going to tell them, tell them the full story with examples and anecdotes, then tell them what you have told them.

6   **Work up to a climax**

Leave your audience with a memorable message and in no doubt about the action you are recommending and what they should do.

 Remember

The best thing to put into your presentation is time. Time to prepare, time to practise and time to set up!

PROBLEM SOLVING

Look for alternatives

Find out the REAL problem. It is not necessarily the obvious problem. There may be historic or personal considerations. (Look out for clues to problems in an organisation such as an increase in absenteeism, uneven production and lateness to work.)

Analyse the problem

Don't make a snap decision about the cause of the problem until you have looked at all the symptoms. Don't rush into defining the problem and trying to solve it immediately. Ask *"Who, what, why, where, when, how and how much?"* And keep asking *"Why?"* and *"What if...?"* Don't blame people; look for weaknesses in systems.

List all possible causes not just the symptoms. Get the facts, then define the problem.

Define the problem

The problem should be defined and stated in short and precise words. The statement should be clear and unambiguous and the results should be able to be measured. *How will we know when we have overcome the problem?*

Brainstorm for possible solutions

Use brainstorming and lateral thinking. Discuss and examine every idea for immediate or future use. Call in experts, look at the problem from different angles and have informal discussions with staff. (See the section on 'Brainstorming')

" Never take your boss a problem unless you can suggest a solution."

Discuss alternative solutions

Consider several possible solutions. Evaluate each solution before you choose the best solution. It may not be ideal, but it could be the one that is least undesirable!

Implement the decision

Explain what has to be done and involve the staff concerned. Set up a timetable and plan the action required to implement it. Decide who does what by when. What will be the implications? Consult people who will be affected by the decision to gain their support.

" How successful was the solution? Follow up and appraise results. Make any changes necessary."

PROBLEM SOLVING

PROBLEM SOLVING

Try a steady approach

Negotiation is often essential when problem solving within an organisation and needs to be handled carefully.

When people are sensitive to delicate issues try a **STEADY** approach.

- **State what you think is the problem.**

  Be courteous and constructive and discuss the issue in a relaxed way.

- **Think about what they say.**

  No matter how defensive their reaction, hear them out. Consider their point of view. What would you do if you were in their situation?

- **Empathise with them.**

  Understanding does not mean agreeing. Say things like, *"I see what you mean."*

- **Ask about alternatives.**

  Pause, and ask them what other ways they have tried to overcome the problem.

  They will tell you why the alternatives didn't work, or wouldn't work. It will help you understand their constraints.

" Most people rush to find solutions before they know what is the real problem."

- **Direct them towards problem solving.**

  Ask them how they would overcome the problem if they could. What are their recommendations? Make suggestions to help them seek a solution.

- **Yield to new ideas.** Involve others in finding an innovative solution.

  Get a commitment to seek a solution to a workplace problem. This is the time to apply some pressure. *"If we cannot come up with a solution we may have to call in an outside consultant."*

PRODUCTIVITY

Increase your output

Productivity is not an end in itself; that end should be customer satisfaction.

To boost productivity in your organisation:

1   **Become a leader who accepts the responsibility of leading teams with vision.**

    Become a leader who can turn customers into partners.

    Be honest, become a good listener and someone who asks key questions.

2   **Hire the best people you can afford.**

    Coach, train and mentor your teams.

3   **Set up an effective performance-based pay plan.**

    Consider paying on results not by the hour.

4   **Move forward with the times.**

    Shed your past. Reduce red tape and bureaucracy in your organisation.

    Reorganise systems for greater efficiency.

    Develop a flexible business.

    Remove ineffective staff or retrain them for more productive tasks.

    Focus on processes to remove long-festering problems.

> " *The greatest setback to productivity is the refusal of staff to accept a goal.* "

5   **Give people the opportunities to perform well.**

    Improve both internal and external communications.

    Make meetings more effective.

    Challenge workers to perform new tasks and take responsibility and initiatives.

    Adopt the motto "Train and gain".

6   **Aim for improved quality.**

    Produce high quality goods the workers are proud of.

    Try setting up a continuous improvement programme.

    Improve your customer service to clients. *"Heed the need for speed."*

PUBLIC RELATIONS

PUBLIC RELATIONS

Get the image you want

It takes time, money and commitment to build a good public image, but it can be lost with one foolish action. The power of public opinion must be faced, understood and dealt with.

To get the public image you want:

Plan and budget your programmes to specific audiences, at selected times.

Set up good two-way communication systems within your organisation.

Tell people about your policies and your activities in a planned objective manner.

Delegate public relations responsibilities to all staff.

Carefully select and train front-line staff and people with extra public relations responsibilities.

Maintain a close liaison with reporters, clients and influential people.

Copy or adapt worthwhile public relations ideas.

Invite objective comments from staff, clients and the audiences you want to reach (your publics).

Investigate complaints fast — be honest, don't make excuses.

To maintain credibility, admit when you have made a mistake.

Listen and respond quickly to the things people are saying about your organisation.

Support high profile 'good causes'.

Repeat your messages in a variety of ways (using mixed media) to produce a stronger community response.

Present your messages attractively. Make them simple, honest and succinct.

" What people say behind your back is your standing in your community."

Planning your public relations programme

1   Set realistic objectives.

2   Define and research your target audiences.

3   Find out their media habits, their knowledge and their views.

    What do they read?

    What radio and television channels do they listen to and watch?

    Where do they get their information from?

4   Analyse what they know, what they want to know, or need to know.

5   Decide on specific messages for each group.

6   Plan the action you propose to take.

7   Prepare a budget.

8   Carry out your plan, adapting and altering it as you get feedback.

9   Review your activities, constantly updating and making changes as necessary.

 Remember

Good public relations does not consist so much in telling the public as in listening to it.

QUALITY

Aim for constant improvement

Quality has more to do with people and their motivation than with equipment and conditions.

Today's quality is tomorrow's reputation.

Principles to remember:

1   Quality is the result of planning, teamwork and a commitment to excellence.

2   Quality can always be improved.

3   Everyone must be encouraged to improve all activities continuously.

4   Quality improves faster if people have a stake in the business.

5   Shifting responsibility from inspectors to workers can cut costs and improve quality.

6   Set quality standards for each step in each job — then aim to improve on them.

7   By continuously making small improvements you can beat the competition.

8   Aim to give the best service, at the lowest price, as fast as possible!

9   Quality should be viewed through the eyes of your customers.

10   Remember if you put your name to a product you should NEVER produce a faulty item!

" Standards will drop unless you refuse to accept anything but the best."

QUESTIONS

Get more information

Most successful people have mastered the art of asking questions. It is a skill worth developing. To gain new knowledge learn to ask specific questions.

Ask open-ended questions

Avoid questions which require a simple *"Yes"* or *"No"* for an answer. Ask open-ended questions to encourage people and help put them at ease. They draw out more information from people.

" Why did you move to the capital?"
" What made you go to Europe?"

Closed questions rarely get more than one or two words in reply.

"Where were you born?"
"How long have you worked here?"

Start with 'comfortable' questions to establish a rapport. Ask about mutual acquaintances, family, hobbies, sports or other interests.

Use key words to get facts — what, why, when , where, who, how and how much.
Kipling's verse is worth memorising.

> *"I keep six honest serving men*
> *(They taught me all I knew) ;*
> *Their names are What and Why and When*
> *And How and Where and Who."*

" Without the right question you will never get the right answer."

Ask 'suppose' questions

"Suppose you were the boss. What things would you change?"

Try 'probe' questions

"You said you were not happy about the job. Why is that?"

Ask 'agreement' questions

"How would it be if we tried such and such?"

Ask for evidence – examples or explanations to discover reasons behind a person's thinking.

"Why did you say that?"
"Give me an example."

✔ *Remember*

To encourage others to think, or to avoid committing yourself to an answer, return the question.

RAPPORT

Ways to establish a rapport with a person

To start a conversation with a stranger it is necessary to go through a kind of ritual. The ritual will vary between races, sexes and the status of people. Here are some basic principles that will help you establish a rapport, in most situations.

- Ask yourself why you want to start a conversation with a person? What is your purpose?

- Get the person talking. Find a common bond of interest. The weather, the temperatures, or the environment are common starting points.

- Try to put the person at ease. Once you have gained the confidence of the other person start asking open-ended questions to find out their interests. *"Do you live around here?" "Do you often come to the football?" "Who do you think is going to win?"*

- Listen carefully, observe the body language and the dress of the other person. Their clothes may tell you something of their lifestyle or interests. Show an interest and try to build the other person's confidence in you.

- Be friendly and natural. Don't argue or monopolise the conversation.

- Try to mirror their behaviour, language and views.

- Once you have established a rapport and found common interests you can ask questions and get information you may not have been able to get before.

- Know when to finish the conversation. End on a positive note in a friendly manner. *"Thank you. I enjoyed our meeting and hearing your views. I hope we meet again soon."*

" You will please more people by listening to them than by talking to them."

RAPPORT

Ways to establish a rapport with an audience

Try to establish a bond with your audience right from the start.

Here are some ways to create a rapport with an audience:

- Before you start speaking take time to compose yourself, nod and smile to someone in the audience.

- An anecdote or a story is a good way to start. Use humour that is pertinent and in good taste, especially if it is at your own expense. Tell a story against yourself, not against others.

- Look for common ground in your opening. Refer to experiences which you have had similar to theirs.

- Quote or indicate your association with people the audience regard highly.

- Focus on their needs not yours. Tell them you agree with some of their hopes, beliefs, attitudes and values. If you are making recommendations explain how these recommendations will help them.

- Be polite and respectful to all present even if you have a hostile audience.

- Show concern, understanding and friendliness towards your listeners.

- Share your feelings and emotions with them.

- If you can identify subgroups in the audience, address them separately. For example if you have a mixed audience, address both the office workers and field workers.

- People are interested in their problems, not in yours.

" Focus on a simple clear message. Work up to a climax - not an anti-climax."

REPORTS

REPORTS

Make recommendations

Report writing can be an interesting and exhilarating experience — it's your chance to help bring about change. It is not a difficult job if first you break it down into small tasks.

Preliminary work

Ask for clear terms of reference!

Who are you doing it for?

Who will read it?

What are the objectives?

How long should the report be?

When is it due?

How much money has been allocated for this work and the printed report?

Where can you collect the background information?

How much help can you expect from other people?

Whom do you need to interview? What are you going to ask them? (Prepare your questions.)

How are you going to record and sort new information?

" Find out everything everybody else knows, and then begin where they left off."

The master plan

Prepare a plan of work to be done.

Set out a realistic timetable for each step of your plan.

Keep to your deadlines.

Researching

Your first task is to collect all the available information from files, libraries, bibliographies, archives, journals, the Internet, CD-ROMs etc. and carry out personal interviews.

Sift the relevant information from the irrelevant — be ruthless but keep a record of references.

Organising your material

When you have collected all the material you require, arrange it in a logical order.

Don't confuse facts and opinions. If it is a fact say so; if it is an opinion assess its value.

Appropriate information goes into the body of the report; relevant supporting material goes into the annex or appendix.

Time is valuable to top management so keep your report brief, to the point, factual and easy to read.

A basic structure for a well set out and comprehensive report:

1 Title

2 Table of contents

3 Abstract (or summary)

4 Introduction

5 Main body

6 Conclusions

7 Recommendations

8 Acknowledgements

9 References

10 Appendices (or annexes)

Title

Make the title factual, clear and brief.

Include key words (for computer reference systems).

Preferably use fewer than 12 words — you can always add a sub-title.

The title page should include details of the author, the name and address of the organisation and the date.

Table of contents

List all the major headings and subheadings, appendices and illustrations with page references.

Abstract (or summary)

Write this last. It is really a mini-report giving the basic facts, the evidence and the conclusions. It should be a single paragraph of approximately 200 words.

Introduction

State the purpose of the report. The introduction usually includes the terms of reference and defines the reasons the report was written.

Main body

It should be easy to read. It should give a comprehensive and systematic review of the subject, the evidence and the possibilities. There should be a logical sequence leading from topic to topic.

Careful paragraphing, subheadings and numbering will help make it easier to read.

Attractive layout creates a good impression and encourages reading.

A suggested layout for the main body of the report:

1.0 MAJOR HEADING

1.1 Subheading

1.1.1 First point

1.1.2 Second point

1.1.3 etc.

1.2 Subheading

2.0 MAJOR HEADING

2.1 Subheading

2.1.1 First point

2.1.2 Second point   and so on...

Conclusions

Busy people may read only the conclusions and recommendations; therefore they should be simple, concise and complete.

The conclusions should be clear statements derived logically from the main body of the report and supported by relevant evidence.

They should be arranged in order of importance and should relate to the purpose of the report.

Recommendations

Recommendations for future action should be stated simply and concisely. Make sure they are positive, practical and cost effective. They should be numbered in order of importance or logic. (They are sometimes put at the beginning of a report.)

Acknowledgements

Thank people or institutions for their help in the preparation of your report. (They are sometimes put before the table of contents.)

References

For books, list:

Author (or authors) : Surname and initials or given name

Year of publication

Title of book

Edition, if applicable

Publisher

Place of publication

International Standard Book Number (ISBN)

Page number or numbers, if applicable.

e.g. Moss, Geoffrey, 1998, Managing for tomorrow,
        Moss Associates Limited,
        Wellington, New Zealand, ISBN 0-9583538-0-8

For journals, list:

Author (or authors): Name first then initials and title

Year of publication

Title of article

Title of journal or periodical

Volume number and part or issue number

Page number or numbers.

Appendices (Annexes)

This section should contain supporting material such as sets of data, details of methods used, graphs and illustrations.

The material should be chosen and presented with the same care and logic as the rest of the report — it is not a dumping ground to fill out a report.

Attractive presentation

Ask a colleague to edit your report — spelling mistakes, lack of logic and verbosity can spoil a report.

An attractive cover and good layout make a favourable first impression.

Follow up

Don't take it for granted the key people will read your report. Take the initiative and make an appointment with them to discuss your findings and to answer questions.

RESTRUCTURING AN ORGANISATION

Increase profitability

After some years in business, most organisations tend to become sluggish. Periodically they need to be redirected and refocused to make them more profitable.

Changes to an organisation require vision, willingness to accept feedback, and decisive action. There are three main stages:

1   Restructuring the organisation

2   Revitalising the business

3   Restoring confidence

I Restructuring the organisation

Start by analysing the present situation

When you have a clear picture of the situation, decide on the changes necessary.

Get your priorities in order and then prepare your action plans.

Focus the company on its core business

Get rid of unprofitable and non-related activities. Revenue from the sale of these activities can be invested in the core business.

Keep the stakeholders informed of proposed changes

Inform interested parties of deficiencies and tell them what actions you are going to take and when you propose to take them. Keep them fully informed, step by step, as the changes unfold. Regular communication is vital!

Reduce and control overheads

An organisation can increase its productivity by cutting costs and reducing waste. Variable costs such as travel, overtime and the costs of raw materials should be investigated.

With improved on-the-job training, staff should be able to perform new tasks and so be more productive. Delegating more efficiently and motivating staff to increase efficiency and production can also save money. (See the sections on DELEGATION and MOTIVATION)

Reducing the number of employees, particularly senior staff, can save money, but be cautious. Do not reduce staff numbers ruthlessly or key staff will start to worry about the security of their own jobs and begin looking for new jobs. Start by not replacing people who retire or leave for personal reasons. If ineffective staff are to have their employment terminated, allow them time to look for alternative jobs, try to find suitable jobs for them outside your organisation or offer them severance pay.

Improve the cash flow

Improve cash flow by negotiating hard with vendors to bring their prices down.

Seek cheaper supplies.

Reduce the volume of stock held by dealing with several competitive 'just-in-time' suppliers.

Collect outstanding debts and insist that customers who are tardy payers pay in advance before delivery.

Make a concerted effort to reduce waste of materials and money. Practice thrift or things will drift! Set a good example and do not indulge in lavish entertainment.

2 Revitalising the business

Re-examine the corporate objectives

If necessary rewrite the company mission statement.

Focus on core business.

Carry out a situation audit and a SWOT analysis. (See CHANGE - Plan for growth)

Conduct market research and an environmental scan and implement aggressive market strategies.

Set up simple financial systems to monitor progress and control waste and inefficiency.

Reduce or eliminate bureaucratic rules.

3 Restoring confidence

Go back to basics

Ask simple questions. "What businesses are we in?" "Why are we in business?" "What do our competitors do better?" "How can we be the best?"

Build a strong corporate culture

Set up rapid two-way communication systems. Keep all staff and people with financial interests informed of developing markets and production situations.

Involve staff in planning and development so they feel they have an input in bringing about changes.

Delegate responsibility to people where the jobs are done.

Treat your staff well and their loyalty and morale will increase.

Develop strong teams with emphasis on a corporate philosophy of constant improvement, service and satisfaction.

" Aim to excel and surpass rivals in all facets of activity."

SELF IMPROVEMENT

Develop new skills

Commit yourself to a life of on-going personal development.

Over the next decade many new skills will be needed. Jobs will go to those who keep updating their education.

Here are ways you can prepare for the future:

1. Keep learning new skills.

2. Build up your self-esteem by accepting new challenges.

3. Join new organisations, make new contacts and build new networks.

4. Attend courses and workshops.

5. Read books and periodicals.

6. Travel to other countries and observe different cultures.

7. Learn foreign languages.

8. Keep looking for new ideas and new information. Experiment and evaluate new experiences.

9. Be curious, constantly seeking new information. Don't take anything for granted. Ask the hard questions.

10. Be prepared to anticipate change, growth, diversification and take-overs.

11. Be ambitious. Try making your dreams come true by breaking them into short-term objectives. Set time limits because people work best when they challenge themselves with deadlines.

SELF IMPROVEMENT

SELF IMPROVEMENT —————————

Identify your needs

Nobody is perfect; we all have our deficiencies. Be prepared to strengthen your weaknesses if you want to succeed in your career.

1   **Check the following lists and identify your weaknesses.**

2   Highlight areas you need to improve.

3   Take one subject at a time and make a planned effort to improve it.

Are you happy with your attitudes and achievements in the following areas?

Achieving, getting things done

Change

Client awareness

Cultural awareness

Delegation

Enthusiasm

Feedback, giving and receiving

Innovation

Interpersonal relationships

Leadership

Managing conflict

Motivation

Staff development

Teamwork

Other...

*" What you want
to be is more
important than
what you are."*

Are you competent in the following areas of knowledge?

Business planning

Commercial judgement

Corporate responsibilities

Cultural responsibilities

Employee relations, race relations etc

Financial management

Global perspective

Health and safety legislation

Management styles

Managing with electronic information systems

Marketing

Media relations

Strategic awareness

Other...

Have you gained and developed skills in the following subjects?

Change management

Coaching

Communication

Computer skills

Counselling

Crisis management

Health and safety practices

Hiring staff and selecting staff for key positions

Leadership

Listening

Managing customer services

Managing quality issues

Marketing

Mentoring

Motivating others

Negotiating

Networking

Organisational management

Performance management

Planning projects

Praising

Presentation

Problem solving

Project management

Public speaking

Questioning

Selling

Team building

Training

Time management

Work reviews

Writing

Others...

Take one subject at a time and make an effort to strengthen that weakness, then concentrate on the next one. You will be surprised how your job satisfaction will increase and your relationships will improve.

" See things as they are and ask 'why?' Dream things as they never were and ask 'why not?'"

SELLING

To sell a product or service

A good salesperson can sell anything because what they are selling is themselves.

Good sellers spend most of their time establishing a rapport with their client. The hard sell comes later, as if doing them a favour.

The best product or service is of little use unless people know about it so marketing, innovation, selling and service all go hand in hand.

Experienced sellers know it is easier to retain existing customers than to find new ones.

The basis for bringing customers back is giving them a great service, unmatched by competitors and by building a trusting relationship.

To be a good seller you must:

" If your website is your shop window, keep changing it!"

- Get to know your product well

- Believe in your product or service

- Believe in yourself

- See many people

- Network by joining many organisations

- Pay attention to timing

- Listen carefully to customers

- Do what is right for your customers

- Develop a sense of humour

- Regularly revisit old customers and friends

- Ask everyone to buy

- Follow up with an after-sales service

- Always exceed the expectations of your clients.

The goal of a seller should be to make life easier for the customer.

SPEECHES ───────────────────────

Analyse your audience

To make an effective presentation you must find out as much as possible about your prospective audience. So before you start preparing your speech, do some research.

Composition of audience

How many will be present?

What is the age range?

Will you be speaking to all women, all men or a mixed audience?

What are their occupations?

What is their economic position?

What is their social status?

What educational levels have they achieved?

What are their racial backgrounds?

Are there any language limitations?

Is the audience derived from a club, an organisation or a specific group?

Beliefs, attitudes and values of members

Will they have strong prejudices?

What are their religious beliefs?

What are their political views?

What are their values?

What are the accepted norms in their social behaviour?

Will they have special interests?

What will motivate them?

> " The first step a speaker should take in preparing for a speech is analysing the audience and the occasion."

The occasion

What is the occasion? Why were you asked?

What are the aims and objectives of the organisation?

What does the audience already know about your subject?

What will be their attitudes towards your views?

What will be their attitudes towards your background and position?

What will they want to hear?

What messages do you want to give them?

SPEECHES

SPEECHES

Keep to the ten commandments

Follow this logical sequence to give a successful speech:

The ten commandments for public speakers

1   Thou shalt think about your topic and your purpose.

2   Thou shalt analyse the audience and the environment.

3   Thou shalt research the topic.

4   Thou shalt create an outline.

5   Thou shalt write drafts and prepare visuals.

6   Thou shalt prepare well, pretest and practise.

7   Thou shalt speak sincerely and confidently.

8   Thou shalt answer questions.

9   Thou shalt evaluate your performance.

10   Thou shalt publicise and follow up.

" Appeal to the
audience's beliefs,
attitudes and
values before you
deliver your
message."

SPEECHES

Plan and practise

If you want your speech to be successful, it must be well prepared and presented confidently.

Follow these guidelines:

1   Analyse your audience.

2   Decide on your objective. (Write it down.) What is your message? What do you want your audience to do?

3   Give your speech a working title.

4   Draft an outline using a clustering method (mind mapping). Usually the main points are sufficient. Jot these down with their supporting statements.

5   Write your speech. Tell your audience something new. Be prepared to write the speech several times until it flows smoothly and sounds right. Write the way you talk not the way you write.

6   Make sure you have a strong conclusion — a summary of what you said or your main point. Make it a climax not an anticlimax!

7   Now write your introduction. Aim to get the attention of your audience. Use it to establish a rapport with them. Tell them what you are going to tell them.

8   Rewrite your title. Make it interesting or intriguing.

9   Edit your speech heavily. Read it aloud. Tape record it and listen carefully. Time it so you will finish within your allocated time.

10   Prepare simple visual aids and handouts.

11   Pick out key memory words in your script and write these on a small card. Use these as your headings to keep you on track.

12   Rehearse your speech until you feel confident using memory card.

" A speech is like a journey. It has purpose, direction and a destination."

SPEECHES
Deliver talks confidently

SPEECHES

1   Dress for your audience. Your clothes should be comfortable and suitable for the occasion.

2   Before the audience arrives, check the sound system and the projectors you will be using for your visual aids. Make sure everyone will be able to see your visual aids. Move to the back of the room to check.

3   Make sure you brief the chairperson about your topic and hand over a copy of your biodata so you can be introduced accurately.

4   When you are introduced and asked to speak, take time to compose yourself. Adjust the microphone and lectern if necessary.

5   Address the chairperson and audience. "Mr Chairman (or Madam Chair), ladies and gentlemen." (If there are any distinguished guests you may need to mention them by name at the start.)

6   Begin with a strong introduction.

7   Use simple, effective visual aids. Do not have too many.

8   Finish with a strong memorable conclusion.

" It's not how long you talk that matters but what you say."

Speech to introduce a speaker

If you are asked to introduce a speaker your role is to create an interest in the topic and the speaker. Tell the audience briefly what the subject is and why the speaker has been chosen to talk about it. You should 'sell' the speaker to the audience. Get your audience interested in the speaker and the topic. Create an atmosphere that will make the speaker want to perform well and the audience keen to listen.

Introduce the audience

As well as introducing the speaker to the audience you should introduce the audience to the speaker. "In this club we have many business leaders and they are keen to hear your ideas on new marketing ventures."

Give qualifications and experience

Tell the audience about the speaker's qualifications, position and title. Don't give a complete biography — just the parts pertinent to the speech, or things that reinforce the authenticity of the subject.

Give the speaker's name as the final part of your introduction.

Make the speaker feel welcome

Lead the applause, keep looking at the speaker and continue clapping until the speaker is ready to begin.

" Be brief, sincere, enthusiastic — and seated."

Recommendations:

Be brief. Be lively. Be sincere.

Don't be over-enthusiastic or too flattering.

Avoid clichés such as 'Today's speaker needs no introduction.'

Don't talk about yourself or your opinions.

Never apologise if your speaker is a substitute for the one you wanted.

Speech to thank a speaker

Speech to thank a speaker

When a guest speaker has addressed a formal meeting, the audience usually show their appreciation by passing a vote of thanks.

Your task is to thank the speaker and to move a vote of thanks.

If the chairperson has asked you earlier if you will move a vote of thanks to the speaker you can be prepared and if necessary make notes during the speech.

At the end of the speech the chairperson will probably give you a nod and you then stand and come forward to the front of the room so all can see you.

Speak up so all can hear you.

"Mr Chairman, I have much pleasure in moving a vote of thanks to Mrs Ross for her interesting talk tonight."

Comment on a few points of interest in the speech and the manner of presentation. Show you enjoyed the speech. Remember you are speaking on behalf of the audience. Be brief, be witty. Thank the speaker sincerely and modestly. Do not criticise the subject matter even if you disagree with it.

Finish with :

"I wish to move a vote of thanks to Mrs Ross."

The chairperson puts the motion to the audience and it is usually 'carried by acclamation' (clapping).

 Remember

Show a lively appreciation of what was said.

Speech to persuade an audience ———

In a persuasive speech, your goal is to influence people so they agree with your argument and take a specific action. Make sure you repeat your argument three times in this type of speech.

1   At the beginning of your speech spend time establishing a rapport with your audience. Look for common ground and concerns. Share your emotions and feelings.

2   Give a quick factual overview of your topic and your views.

3   Explain the need or the problem. Dramatise your presentation. How does it affect them?

4   Give your solution for meeting the need or overcoming the problem. Explain why you think it is the best solution.

5   Show how your ideas will work. Reinforce your message with facts, a demonstration or by using convincing visual aids.

6   Tell them again how they will benefit.

7   Explain what action they need to take.

8   Conclude with a memorable summary. Urge them to support your point of view or take a specific action.

 Remember

Your final statement should be a climax not an anticlimax.

Speech to propose a toast

The formal toast is a call to people to drink in honour of a person or persons or to an institution.

If you are toasting the head of state (the loyal toast) the correct procedure is *"The Queen"* or *"The President"*, and nothing more.

If it is a personal toast, make sure you get the person's name and title correct. When you are called to propose the toast, rise slowly and wait until the audience is quiet. (If people continue to talk, tap your glass with a spoon to get their attention.)

When you are ready, start slowly and strongly.

"Mr Chairman, distinguished guests and fellow members"

(or whatever is appropriate for the occasion). If you have important people in your audience, you may need to mention them by name.

The toast should be brief — three to five minutes is usually long enough. You may need some brief headings written on a small card for this speech. Remember you should express respect and admiration for the person or persons being honoured.

Keep eye contact with your audience as much as possible but turn to the person or persons being honoured from time to time as you mention their achievements. You can use humour in this speech but if you are not a good storyteller keep to personal anecdotes.

Finish your speech with a message of goodwill to the honoured guest or guests.

Face your audience and if they are seated ask them to rise. (Make sure you have sufficient liquid in your glass to drink the toast.) Give them time to stand, then...

"Raise your glasses and drink the toast to our honoured guests."
"To our guests!"

STAFF APPRAISALS

Know your employees

Appraisals should be informal coaching sessions held regularly to encourage, to stimulate and to inform. The person carrying out the appraisal has the role of counsellor.

A staff appraisal should:

- Help employees do a better job.
- Stimulate self-development.
- Prepare people for future job opportunities.
- Seek honest feedback about the work and look for ways to improve output and working conditions.
- Foster better personal relations.
- Encourage high standards of performance.
- Let people know where they stand in the organisation.
- Set agreed work objectives.
- Review salary and organisational work incentives.

Helpful hints:

Start an appraisal by discussing progress made and successes achieved. Focus on a person's strengths and accomplishments - not on their weaknesses!

Employees want to know:

'How well am I doing?'

'How can I do a better job?'

'What do I need to do to earn more money?'

'Where can I go from here?'

'What are my long term prospects?'

Be honest with people. You will not help them by hiding the truth. Criticism should always be constructive and helpful.

Encourage them to contribute ideas.

" Take care not to make promises you cannot keep."

Together produce a plan for their future development.

Use a system of mutual goal-setting.

Keep the plan simple and feasible and focus on short-term activities.

Arrange any future training needed to achieve goals. Recommendations to overcome weaknesses should be specific and realistic in terms of what, when, where, and how things are to be done.

Ask questions :

'Are you happy working here?'

'What jobs do you like doing best?'

'What problems have you had recently?'

'Are there any procedures we should review? Why do you think that?'

'Is there anything in your job description that has become redundant or you wish to change?'

'Can I do anything to help you do a better job?'

'Am I doing anything that hinders your work?'

'How could your job or the organisation be improved?'

'Have you any ideas how we could improve our staff communications?'

'What do you see as your key strengths and weaknesses?'

'Where do you see your future in this organisation?'

'What do you hope to achieve during the next month?'

'What training would you like to help you meet your goals and ambitions?'

" People must always understand clearly what is expected of them and how well they are performing. "

'If I could do one thing to help you do a better job, what would that be?'

STAFF SELECTION

Recruit the best

Successful selection starts well before the interview. Recruit staff with skills needed to strengthen your organisation. Aim to build a team whose members have different skills.

Before an interview

Write a job description. What work do you expect the person to do ? List tasks, working conditions, responsibilities, relationships, designation, etc.

Next list personal qualities needed for the job — appearance, health, knowledge and skills, intelligence, expectations and values etc. (Write down the topics you want to cover in the interview.) Where appropriate devise short tests of relevant skills.

Select a pleasant quiet room for the interview. Minimise disturbances — put a 'Meeting in progress' sign on the door and stop all telephone calls. Before the interview, while the candidates are waiting, arrange for someone to look after them. Make them feel welcome. Perhaps your receptionist could give them a cup of coffee and talk to them.

At the interview

When they enter the interview room, introduce them to other people in the room and make them feel at ease. Make small talk and let them relax before you move into the serious interview.

" You are only as good as the staff you recruit."

Ask questions in everyday language. Get the candidate talking by asking open-ended questions or inviting comments. "Tell us what you have done since you left school." Encourage the candidate to ask questions about the job or organisation, but don't lose control of the interview. Working conditions should be clearly explained and understood. Make notes after each interview.

Never let a candidate leave an interview feeling demoralised even if they are unsuitable. They should be told they lack the skills required in a way that maintains their self-respect.

After the interview

Decide on an appointment as soon as possible. If you need to check any details, use the telephone — it's surprising what people will tell you over the telephone. Contact the successful applicant with a job offer. Find out when they can start work.

Thank the unsuccessful applicants as soon as possible and keep a list of their names and addresses in case you need them later.

STROKE

Reduce tension and worry

When your body tells you are under stress, it is time to review your lifestyle. Try to think through the causes of your stress. They may be pressure of work, a difficult boss, marital problems, financial worries, peer pressures or other reasons.

Before you make any vital decisions, try to go for a relaxing holiday — forget about work for a while. Be prepared to reorganise your lifestyle. You may need to change your environment — your job, your town or city. You may need to get away from your peers if their social pressures are too great. You may need to change your accommodation if it is unsatisfactory or too far from your work.

Make time to relax. Take control of your life and plan time for periods of leisure.

Exercise regularly. If you are not an active sportsperson, follow a sport you enjoy watching. Get out in the fresh air.

Make an effort to have fun.

Do more of the things you enjoy doing most.

Keep healthy. Make sure you have a sensible, healthy diet.

Learn relaxation methods to ease tense muscles.

Aim for moderation in all things.

" The bow too tensely strung is easily broken."

Ways to overcome stress

Review your private life

If you have a job you don't enjoy or are in an unsatisfactory relationship look for other alternatives.

Try to socialise regularly and maintain a network of friends.

Maintain interests apart from your work.

Talk about your problems and feelings with someone you confide in.

Give and receive affection.

Make time for things you really enjoy.

Practical solutions:

Plan and organise your time better. Set limits to what you are prepared to do. Learn to say "No" if people make too many demands on your time.

Have fun. Enjoy your work. Try not to take your work too seriously.

Share the burden of responsibility with others in your organisation.

Don't become a perfectionist. Set a high standard and when that is reached, move on to the next task.

Learn to delegate tasks to people you can trust.

Have a hobby or a sporting interest. Play cards or board games, bowls or pool for pleasure. Take up gardening. Enjoy good relaxing music.

Join organisations such as a drama club, music group, film club, gardening club etc.

Go swimming, tramping, skiing or engage in similar outdoor activities.

Watch television for relaxation.

Personal responsibilities:

Make sure you get enough sleep.

Exercise regularly.

Eat the right foods. (Your diet should include plenty of fruit, vegetables and complex carbohydrates. Reduce the intake of fats, sugar and salt.) Have a good breakfast. Eat moderately — don't have large meals.

Watch your weight. (Try to maintain an acceptable weight for your age and height.)

Preferably, no smoking. (If you are a smoker, reduce the number of cigarettes and seek help to overcome this addiction.)

Restrict your intake of coffee and alcoholic drinks. 'Moderation in all things' is good advice to follow.

Have regular medical and dental checks, and eyesight and hearing tests if necessary.

Look beyond physical causes of stress:

Reflect on the spiritual side to life. Develop a sound philosophy based on qualities such as honesty and sincerity.

Plan a quiet time each day to think and read, meditate, practise yoga or Tai Chai.

Go for walks to relax, to think and for exercise to help you sleep.

Be optimistic and enthusiastic about your work and life.

Look for the good in people. Be friendly, compassionate and helpful.

If you fail to overcome your stress problems seek counselling and professional advice. There are some excellent stress management programmes so don't hesitate to ask for help.

Overcoming stress at work:

To help overcome work-related stress, make an effort to get organised. Read Chapter One and try putting some of the recommendations into practice.

Here are some basic principles:

1 Plan your work thoroughly. Allow time for interruptions and thinking time.

2 Learn to decline jobs when people ask you to take on extra duties.

3 Delegate responsibilities to people you can trust. (See the section on 'Delegation')

4 Set realistic goals and objectives. Many people make the mistake of being too ambitious.

5 Solve problems as soon as you have all the facts. Learn to make decisions quickly.
   Don't procrastinate!

6 Meet deadlines early so there are no last-minute panics. Eliminate perfectionism.

7 Learn to handle pressure and emergencies calmly. Try to control your anger when provoked.

 Remember

The best way to reduce stress is to do the things you enjoy doing.

8   Work hard for limited periods. Try to complete what you have planned for each day. Do not take work home!

9   Plan for breaks during the day. Don't work through your lunch time. Get away from the office — go for a walk or a jog.

10 Ways to reduce your stress

1   Organise yourself and plan your work and leisure.

2   Make decisions quickly and meet deadlines early.

3   Delegate responsibilities to people you can trust.

4   Take time out to get your work in perspective.

5   Reward yourself when you have done a good job.

6   Learn to relax and control your anger if things go wrong.

7   Keep healthy with a balanced diet and sensible exercise.

8   Set aside time each week for leisure and things you enjoy.

✓ *Remember*

A relaxed approach can add years to your life.

9   Balance your lifestyle. Be moderate in all things.

10   Be aware of what your body is telling you. Seek help if necessary.

SUCCESS

Plan for a successful career

Success in the world of business, artistic achievement or other aspects of life depends on talent, ambition, imagination and much hard work.

Believe in yourself. If your goals are realistic, you can achieve most things you want in life.

Concentrate on the things you do best and further develop your talents.

Build up your confidence and your self-esteem.

Accept new responsibilities and new challenges.

Break your dreams and aspirations up into short-term objectives.

Set time limits to achieve your objectives.
People work best when they have to meet realistic deadlines.

Tell people about your deadlines.
Once you have committed yourself to meet a deadline, you are more likely to achieve it.

Acknowledge your strengths and weaknesses and work to overcome the weaknesses.

Be optimistic and forward thinking.
Always try to look on the positive side of things.

Be prepared to take risks.
Don't be afraid to fail. Failure is a learning experience.

Look for basic principles and common truths in your daily life.
Try to rid yourself of clutter. Don't waste your time and effort on unimportant things.

Constantly seek new information.
Be curious. Question all major decisions. Don't take anything for granted. Learn to ask simple basic questions - *what, why, when, where, how, how much, and how do you know?*

Take full responsibility for all your decisions.

Earn a reputation for meeting deadlines and getting things done.

Be honest and modest.

Treat other people, as you would like them to treat you.

Never undermine the ability of others - everyone wants to succeed.

Find a job you enjoy.
People do best what they enjoy doing.

Keep up-to-date with your skills and add new ones. Read, study, network, train and travel.

Learn the skills of effective communication.
Learn to write simple, clear and concise letters, reports and e-mails. Learn to chair and address a meeting. Learn presentation skills.

Manage your time firmly.
Don't let others waste your time. However, allow time to make new friends, network, study and learn new skills. Make sure you spend quality time with your family.

✓ *Remember*

Your success can help many people. Your failure helps no one.

Build financial independence.
Invest a percentage of your income each pay day. Plan for a time when you cannot work to generate an income. *(See MONEY — Sound investing)*

Think globally and look to the future.
Learn from the past but watch out for new trends. They bring new opportunities!

Be kind to yourself.
Reward your successes and achievements by taking time off to relax, to socialise, and to have fun.

" If you want to be a success in business, look for new paths. Don't travel the worn paths of others."

Be generous and compassionate.
Give some time and money for the less fortunate people of this world.

Happiness and satisfaction in life depend largely upon what we do for others.

SUPERVISION

Be a team leader

In the past, supervisors in organisations were controllers of activities. In today's work climate, the supervisor is being replaced by the team leader who delegates control to others and becomes the coordinator.

An autocratic supervisor must be retrained to become a democratic leader. A good supervisor knows how to involve staff in team efforts, pays attention to details and standards, and is able to delegate responsibility to others.

Many organisations are functioning somewhere between controlled supervision and democratic work teams but the basic principles still apply.

Principles of good supervision:

1   Employees must always understand clearly what is expected of them.

2   They must have guidance in doing their work and know who they can go to for advice.

3   Good work should always be praised or rewarded in public.

4   Poor work should be criticised constructively, away from the hearing of other people.

5   People should have opportunities to show they can accept greater responsibilities.

6   People should be encouraged to improve themselves.

7   People should work in a safe and healthy environment.

*" Do as you would
be done by."*

Good bosses tell their employees:

1   What is expected of them.

2   To whom they are responsible.

3   How they are performing.

4   How they can improve.

TEAMS

Build strong groups

Teams are set up in organisations so groups of people with the necessary skills can work together towards a common goal. Different tasks require different types of teams. Before you set up a team, you must have a clear objective.

Kinds of Teams:

Do you want a team to:

Run things?

To solve problems and make recommendations?

To make things, or carry out specific tasks?

There are three main types of teams:

1   **Management teams** coordinate and run things.

2   **Problem-solving teams**, task forces or committees are set up to make recommendations.

3   **Work teams** (ideally self-managed teams) have specific responsibilities for producing things or providing services.

" Teamwork is less 'me' and more 'we'. "

Other types of teams include:

Quality circles which are set up to search for ways to increase productivity and improve quality and **Virtual teams** whose members communicate by computer and take turns at leading.

TEAMS

Select with care

The success or failure of most organisations will depend on whether people work together effectively in teams.

To get greater synergy:

1   Select compatible, competent team members and enthusiastic leaders.

2   Tell them you expect high standards.

3   Spell out the rules and the roles.

4   Give realistic challenges and set clear goals.

5   Discuss your problems and concerns.

6   Set deadlines but allow time for team building.

7   Encourage imagination, initiative and free speech.

8   Make teams accountable for their work.

9   Praise successes.

10 Reward teams for good work.

Few organisations are skilled at making teams work together with other teams.

" Small streams join to form mighty rivers."

Managers must work hard and show diplomacy to bring teams together to focus on single targets.

TEAMS

Rules for success

TEAMS

1   Choose a leader with the skills to lead and develop a productive team and one who can facilitate problem solving.

2   Choose members who have the qualifications to make a balanced team.

3   The members must be committed to the aims of the team.

4   Develop a climate in which people feel relaxed, able to express their personal views, carry out free discussion and if necessary, take risks.

5   Give the team clear, worthwhile and challenging objectives.

6   Teams should be involved in corporate planning and feel they are contributing to the organisation.

7   Teams should develop effective work methods and systematic and effective ways to solve problems together. Roles should be clearly defined and results well documented.

" The only way to judge a team is by results."

8   There should be plenty of time permitted for a team to develop, to discuss, comment and evaluate problems objectively without rancour, criticism or personal attacks.

9   The teams should feel free to create new ideas and to take risks — and be rewarded if their good ideas are adopted.

10 There should be regular social and reporting contacts with other teams in the organisation.

TEAMS

Reasons for failure

The two most likely causes of team failure are lack of time and lack of feedback.

Some teams fail, or do not perform to their full potential, for the following reasons:

1   Insufficient time was allowed to build an effective team.

2   There were unrealistic or unclear goals and objectives.

3   The team thinks its task not worthwhile.

4   The team leader is not accepted by the other members.

5   The leader proves to be incompetent for the task.

6   The team becomes disenchanted because of lack of feedback, both positive and negative.

7   The team is given little credit for their achievements.

8   Some individuals resist team work or are incompatible with other members, and sabotage the efforts of the team.

" Failure is the path of least persistence."

TEAMS

Improve their performance

At the start, each team must know exactly what it is expected to do.

It must be given clear guidelines in line with the goals of the organisation.

Have patience when teams are first set up. Let them work out their own strategies to achieve their objectives.

They must be given authority and made accountable.

Others must be told about the formation of a new team, its membership, its objectives, its role in the organisation and who its members are responsible to.

To improve teams:

1   Use your enthusiasm and vision to encourage them right from the start.

2   Train teams to use techniques to stimulate innovative thinking. Encourage them to use brainstorming, buzz groups, mind mapping and other techniques to generate new ideas and to promote free discussion.

" Give teams your support, encouragement and praise."

3   Regular reporting, feedback, support and constant encouragement are essential.

4   Report on actions taken on their recommendations and the results achieved.

5   Reward teams for their successes and contributions. Reward the whole team, not just the leader.

TELECONFERENCING ————————

Save travel time and expenses

Teleconferences are valuable in improving communications in organisations working in distant locations. They save time and money by eliminating the need to travel, but they must be planned well.

Requirements:

1   A prepared agenda. Don't be too ambitious. Keep to a simple agenda.

2   A budget. Know how much money is available and how much you expect to spend.

3   Make special arrangements with your local telecommunications organisation.

4   A facsimile machine is essential as a support tool.

5   A quiet, disturbance-free room, with suitable telephone lines and equipment.

6   The floor should be carpeted and the walls should be curtained to stop echoing.

7   A convenor who organises the teleconference and acts as a facilitator. At each location there should be a meeting leader skilled in controlling groups.

8   An extra telephone line in each location for technical control. In a multi-location conference only one location should be responsible for re-establishing faulty connections.

" Planning, preparation and follow-up are the keys to a successful teleconference."

Helpful hints:

The agenda should be negotiated well in advance of the meeting. The more specific the agenda the more effective the meeting will be. Background papers should be sent by facsimile well in advance of the meeting.

Put a notice on the teleconference room door to stop interruptions and instruct the telephone operators not to put local calls through to participants during your teleconference.

Explain the ground rules and start with introductions.

Tell all present they are expected to take part in discussions.

Speak slowly and clearly in global English.

Keep your messages concise and to the point. Don't give too many details. You can say *"I will send you a copy of my full report".*

Check to see your messages are being understood. Ask leading questions, such as *"What will happen in your country if you were to carry out my recommendations?" (NOT, 'Did you understand that?')*

The local facilitator's job is to involve the quiet and control the dominant speakers.

Say *"What do Lou and Alice think about that idea? They have had experience working on this type of project in Asia last year."*

Make brief notes during the teleconference to keep track of the discussion, to get names right and to jog your memory.

If you are taking a vote don't say *"All in favour say aye."* Say *"Who disagrees with the proposition?"*

Minutes should be sent to each location by facsimile as soon as possible after the meeting, with any handouts covered during the discussions.

If action was agreed upon, the name or the names of the persons responsible for tasks should be included in the minutes. Be specific, give commitments, time and dates tasks are to be completed.

The convenor's checklist:

Tick when done

1 Purpose. What do you expect to achieve? (Write it down.) ❏

2 Who will participate? What locations? ❏

3 Who will be the leaders in each location? ❏

4 Negotiate proposed dates and a suitable time. ❏

5 Negotiate the agenda. (Not too many agenda items.) ❏
   Time meeting will start
   Rules and procedures
   Introductions and purpose
   Agenda items in priority order
   Summaries and reviews
   Follow-ups
   Time meeting will finish

6 Are background papers and equipment needed? ❏

7 Do you want minutes or published proceedings ❏
   following the meeting? (If so, you will need to appoint
   reporters and organise the production and the
   distribution of the minutes or proceedings.)

TELEPHONING

TELEPHONING

Try these tips

To save time and make better use of your telephone:

Keep a list of frequently called numbers handy to your telephone. Make use of your telephone memory and automatic re-dial buttons.

You can take notes when you talk if you use a hands-free telephone or a shoulder-fitting device which clamps to your telephone handset.

A telephone answering tape recorder can record messages for you. With some machines you can receive your messages when you are travelling by dialling your home telephone number and using a code number.

Business calls should be planned

Before you place a call, list the points you want to cover or questions you want to ask.

Impressions depend entirely on what is heard

Smile before you talk and try to sound friendly and enthusiastic.

" The telephone is one of the most effective time-savers and one of the biggest time-wasters."

Perceptive listening is important

Listen for voice tone and inflections, to tell if your contact sounds busy or preoccupied. If so, offer to call back.

Don't do all the talking

Pause from time to time. Give the other person time to think and respond.

Call your contact by name

If in doubt, ask the telephone operator the name of the person you will be talking to.

Make your calls at convenient times

Get to know people's work habits. For international calls, allow for differences in time zones and daylight saving times.

When calling long distance

Tell the operator who answers where you are calling from. This encourages prompt action. Keep frequently used references handy to the telephone. If an inward call requires further research, don't keep the caller waiting. Offer to locate the information and phone back at a specific time.

If clients call with complaints

Be sympathetic — do not cover up with excuses. Thank them for bringing the problem to your notice and offer to investigate and call back. Investigate as soon as possible, phone back and explain what you are going to do about the problem.

When selling over the telephone

1   Identify yourself and your organisation.

2   Establish a rapport.

3   State the purpose of your call and how the product will be to their advantage.

4   Arrange a personal visit or demonstration.

5   Conclude on a friendly note.

Involve your switchboard operator

Switchboard operators are usually the first contacts people have with your organisation. They are very important people. Train them well. Keep them informed of staff responsibilities, dates, times and places of meetings, names of publications and activities of the office or department. The more you involve them the easier they will make your job.

Keep the operator informed of your movements

If you cannot be found when an important long-distance call comes through you could lose business. Make sure your operator has your cell phone number handy.

TELEVISION

Guidelines for interviews

The essence of television is entertainment. If a programme lacks drama, human interest, humour or tragedy, you won't get air time.

If you have a choice, take the risk and choose a live interview (one which goes on air as you speak) rather than a pre-recorded interview. A pre-recorded video film can be cut and edited down to a brief clip and could be used out of context. This puts you at a disadvantage if your opponent is asked to comment on selected statements.

If a camera team comes to your office to interview you, move away from your desk. Set up some easy chairs or stand in front of a backdrop. Sitting behind a desk makes you look intimidating.

Some reporters will deliberately let interviews go on for a long time in the hope you will let your guard down and say something controversial or colourful. Be careful what you say. Remember the reporter is simply trying to make interesting and lively television for viewers.

Take time to think when asked a difficult question. In a pre-recorded interview pauses can be edited out.

Give honest direct answers. If you don't know — say so. *"No comment"* is interpreted as *"You are right, but I am not prepared to confirm it".*

" There are two kinds of people who do not say much — those who are quiet, and those who talk too much."

Hints for television appearances:

Wear light-weight clothes for the heat of the studio. Avoid bold patterned clothes. A pastel-coloured shirt or blouse looks better than a white one.

Don't drink alcohol before an interview — your viewers will be able to tell.

Sit up straight in your chair — don't slump.

Look at the interviewer — don't look at the floor or the ceiling for inspiration.

Start strongly with plenty of energy.

Be enthusiastic. You must appear lively and excited about your topic.

Be credible. Speak with confidence and authority.

Talk conversationally, but convincingly and persuasively.

Be yourself — as natural as possible. Don't answer in an official manner. Don't sound like a bureaucrat! Try to be sincere and informal. Speak in *'thoughts'* — in groups of words, not in sentences — 'talk stuff' not 'book stuff'.

Share your feelings and emotions with your viewers. Smile only when appropriate. A nervous smile at the wrong time can send the wrong message to viewers.

The interviewer's job is to get you to answer the questions in the minds of the viewers. Try to answer briefly and honestly — don't ramble on. An interviewer will apply pressure if you try to evade questions.

Don't hesitate to correct your interviewer if you are being misrepresented. Your job is to present facts, to add to or to interpret information. You may have to correct misapprehensions if you are discussing topical or controversial issues. Keep control of the interview. Try to retain your sense of humour even when you are provoked.

Remain calm under all circumstances.

Try to avoid speech mannerisms, especially jargon and clichés, such as *'at this point in time'*, *'but first I would like to say'* and *'I think'*.

Your viewers will remember the way you react and the overall impression you make, rather than what you say.

Your final statement is the one they are most likely to remember.

Finish on a strong note with a succinct summary!

THINKING TIME

THINKING TIME

Make time to plan

Successful businesses are based on ambition, imagination and planning. They create a work environment for people to think, plan and experiment with new ideas. Good ideas need to be well thought through - they need 'incubation' time.

People involved in management, research and many other careers need time to be alone, time to think and space to try things out.

Make time to think

- Slow your pace down.

- Plan each day and set aside a time to read and think.

- At the end of the day, plan the following day's programme.

- Get up early so you have time to exercise, go for walk or at least have a leisurely breakfast.

- Arrive early at work, when things are quiet.

- If you have a difficult project, research the subject and make notes of your ideas.

- Turn off your pager or cell phone when you are thinking and planning.

" The way you think determines the way you act. And the way you act will decide your future."

To help you think clearly

- Meditate or practise yoga or tai chi to help you relax.

- Listen to soothing music.

- Take a relaxing holiday.

- Go fishing, tramping, climbing or swimming or relax away from crowds and the pressure of work.

- Attend learning workshops, study groups and seminars to hear about new ideas.

- Travel to other places to see what others do. This allows you to think and to get your life in some perspective.

- Make time to enjoy your family and think about their future.

TIME-SAVING TIPS

Be efficient in the office

Good working habits can save you much time and effort.

❖ Are you sure you know what your job really is — your responsibilities and your duties? If you are not sure, get them redefined.

❖ Take a check on your work load — list unessential jobs and time-wasting procedures.

❖ Become conscious of time, without undue anxiety.

❖ Constantly plan your work.

❖ Strive for goals and objectives.

❖ Look for techniques that best suit your style of work.

❖ Cut 'red tape' to the minimum.

❖ Identify your peak working hours and use them well.

❖ Commit yourself to responsible tasks.

❖ Try to get your priorities right — important jobs first.

❖ Practise making fast decisions.

❖ Don't become a perfectionist.

❖ Sift and sort inward mail fast, into priority order.

❖ Action a letter the first time you pick it up. Try to respond to all messages within 24 hours of receiving them.

❖ Keep model letters for routine replies.

❖ Learn to dictate.

❖ Computerise lists for commonly used addresses.

❖ Index frequently used fax and telephone numbers.

❖ Keep your desk clear of clutter.

❖ Don't file useless information.

❖ Develop a reliable filing and bring-up system.

❖ Try to complete one job at a time.

 Remember

To save time and effort, don't put things down, put them away.

❖ Don't put jobs off — complete them as soon as you have the facts.

❖ To overcome procrastination, break big jobs into segments, set deadlines, tell people about them and start.

❖ Develop systematic habits.

❖ List working procedures, rules and policies to be followed.

❖ Learn to read fast and efficiently.

❖ Identify information-rich sources and use abstracting and review services.

❖ Use checklists and reminder lists.(Use this book!)

" Waste no time in vain regrets."

TRAINING

Aim for results

The aim of training should be to inspire action rather than fill with knowledge.

Involve learners in their own training by letting them set their own goals and encouraging them to share their work experiences. Train and develop staff by taking every opportunity for them to learn new skills.

Training programmes need careful planning and preparation if they are to be successful.

The Trainer's ABCD:

A **Audience.** Who are you going to train? Be specific.

B **Behaviour.** What type of change do you expect?

C **Condition.** When and under what conditions do you expect this change to occur?

D **Degree.** How much change do you expect and how will you find out?

Steps in a training programme:

1 Analyse the job.

2 Analyse the trainees.

3 Assess the training needs.

4 Set training objectives.

5 Select and organise the content of your programme.

6 Select training techniques, methods, aids.

7 Prepare lesson plans.

8 Decide how the programme is to be evaluated.

9 Carry out training.

10 Evaluate.

11 Review the programme and revise if necessary.

" Training should be linked to real work situations and should include creative and lateral thinking ."

Planning is the key to success

1 Job analysis

Describe the job. What qualifications does the worker need to do the job?

What does the worker do?

Why?

How?

How well?

2 Trainee analysis

Who are they? What can they do already?

Where are they?

What are their special characteristics?

What level of knowledge / skills / experience do they have?

3 Training needs assessment

What are their weaknesses? How can you help them overcome these weaknesses?

List weaknesses and ways of overcoming them.

4 Determine training objectives

These describe what trainees should be able to do at the end of their training that they could not do previously.

An objective must:

Describe the final results

Be specific and precise

Describe a change that is measurable or observed

List criteria against which success can be measured

Mention essential conditions under which results can be achieved

Specify an end point.

What change do you want? When do you want it? How much change? How will you know?

What has to be done?

Under what conditions?

Up to what standards?

How will it be evaluated?

5   Select and organise content

Study the background information.

Decide on the content of the training programme.

Organise the content in logical order.

6   Select training techniques, methods, aids

Decide which training techniques, methods and aids will best suit your topic.

Select the most appropriate methods for the educational level of your trainees.

Decide on the best training aids required for the work environment.

7   Prepare lesson plans

Allocate how you are going to use your time and step by step activities.

Decide on how each lesson is to be presented.

Set out each lesson step by step.

Allocate time for each activity.

8   Plan evaluation

A good evaluation will help you do better next time.

Decide on the information required.

Decide when this should be collected.

Study methods of gathering information.

Select method to be used.

Prepare questions which have to be answered.

9 Conduct training

Encourage participation and use a variety of training methods.

Keep to your lesson plans.

Use a variety of methods.

Encourage participation.

Use demonstrations, models, visual aids.

10 Evaluate training

Make sure you get honest feedback.

Conduct the planned evaluation.

Summarise results.

Write your evaluation report.

11 Review and revise

 *Remember*

Always strive to do better next time.

Summarise training.

Review in the light of your evaluation.

Discuss with other trainers involved.

Revise to improve relevance.

TRAINING

Evaluate yourself as a trainer

How good are you as a trainer? Read the following questions.
Tick if you believe you are doing a good job.

DO YOU —

❏ Assess the general standard of learning and knowledge of your trainees so that you can begin at an appropriate level?

❏ Plan and develop every training programme to suit the varied needs of the group members?

❏ Present well-organised sessions?

❏ State the objective of the training?

❏ Explain any changes you intend to make and give reasons for the changes?

❏ Make enthusiastic statements about the course and discuss expectations with participants?

❏ Involve participants right from the start?

❏ Start with a topic familiar to the group, but add something new to stimulate curiosity and arouse awareness of previously unrecognised needs?

❏ Move forward one step at a time?

❏ Adjust the size and difficulty of each step to the learners' ability?

❏ Adjust each step, not only to the group as a whole, but to individuals in the group?

❏ Build each step on the preceding step?

❏ Point out what was important to learn in each session?

❏ Give step by step instructions in writing, when needed?

" It's harder to unlearn than learn."

❏ Make sure you provide opportunities for all members to practise their newly-acquired skills?

❏ Relate course materials to real life situations?

❏ Use relevant examples to help make points?

❏ Set exercises that are worthwhile and relevant with useful practical recommendations?

❏ Use a variety of teaching techniques?

❏ Use a variety of teaching materials and different types of visual aids?

❏ Summarise often?

❏ Review at the beginning and the end of each session?

❏ Set up challenging and competitive group situations?

❏ Encourage unresponsive trainees to participate?

❏ Make every member feel involved and feel they can share experiences freely without loss of face?

❏ Initiate conversations with participants before and after sessions?

❏ Address each person by name?

❏ Praise students during sessions?

❏ Encourage thinking and the use of imagination in your exercises?

❏ Carry out simple recall exercises?

❏ Allow sufficient time for creative thinking to produce worthwhile ideas?

❏ Set challenging assignments?

❏ Work participants hard for specific periods, never for indefinite periods?

❏ Set deadlines and keep to them?

❏ Make written comments on assignments?

❏ Encourage research and public reporting back to the group?

❏ Give brief, factual handouts?

❏ Develop a working climate which encourages constructive self-criticism?

❏ Carry out regular evaluations of:

   the course content?

   the curriculum?

   your effectiveness as a tutor?

❏ Keep up-to-date with new techniques and training tools by reading, researching and attending conferences, seminars and training workshops?

❏ Experiment with new training methods?

HOW CAN YOU IMPROVE?

Look at all the questions you have not ticked. These are your training weaknesses. (Mark these with a highlight pen.)

Make a real effort to work on these areas. Tackle them one at a time and plan how you can improve as a trainer.

1 Decide which one you will deal with first.

2 Make an action plan.

3 Start at your next training session.

4 Keep to your plan.

5 Evaluate your performance during sessions and at the end of each session. Don't look for an ego boost, look for ways to improve.

6 How can you do a better job next time?

7 Keep trying.

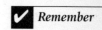 **Remember**

Practice is the best master.

TRAINING WAYS

Use imagination and a variety of methods to make training enjoyable and participative.

Here are some commonly used training ways:

Audience reaction team
Brainstorming
'Buzz' session
Case study
Committee
Conference
Convention
Debate
Demonstration
Discussion group
Drama spots — role playing
Exercise or assignment
Exhibit or display
Field trip
Film
Forum
Interview
Lecture
Listening team
Multi-media package
Panel
Peer teaching
Programmed instruction
Question time or quiz
Seminar
Short course
Skit
Symposium
Teleconference
Tour
Video-television
Visit
Workshop
  and so on...

" Variety is the spice of life."

Which training methods should you use ?

Variety is important but some methods are more suitable than others. Your decision will depend on what you are trying to teach and on the educational level of your participants.

To transfer knowledge, use:

Group discussions (questions and answers)
Group or individual exercises
Lectures (with handouts)
Forums
Panel discussions
Films, videos etc.

To solve problems, use:

Case studies
Brainstorming
Discussion groups
Exercises etc.

To develop skills, use:

Demonstrations for manual skills
Role playing for interpersonal skills
Peer teaching
Programmed instruction etc.

To change attitudes, use:

Debates
Displays
Role playing (for clarifying how others feel)
Group discussions (for group attitudes)
Individual exercises
Demonstrations
Campaigns etc.

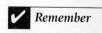 **Remember**

Returns from learning should be more earnings.

TRAVEL

Tips for trips

Research and plan your trip by talking to people who have travelled in the countries you hope to visit. Always deal with an experienced, well-established travel agent.

Make sure your passport is valid for at least six months from the date of your departure. Obtain any necessary visas and check that vaccinations are up to date. It is advisable to have travel insurance so you are covered for unpredictable circumstances.

Find out about the seasonal climate at your destination. This is especially important if you are visiting areas with a monsoon climate. Spring is often a good time to visit in temperate regions. Write your own checklist of essentials to pack — clothes, toilet gear, medication, camera etc.

Here is a suggested checklist:

This will vary depending on countries you will visit and the standard of your accommodation.

Suits (mix and match)

Comfortable clothes for lounging

" Take twice as much money as you think you will need and half as many clothes."

Shirts or blouses

Ties

Underclothes

Socks (cotton for hot climates)

Comfortable shoes, sandals and shoe cleaning items

Nightwear, swimwear, rainwear (umbrella)

Handkerchiefs and /or tissues

Toilet requisites (toothbrush etc.), cosmetics

Small medical kit with essential medicines or pills (carry emergency prescriptions)

Torch

Travel alarm clock

Small radio (to pick up BBC international news in foreign countries)

Diary, maps ,stationery

Plastic bags (and rubber bands) for dirty clothes, shoes, keeping ants out of foodstuff etc.

Camera and films

Small electric jug with multi-plug for boiling water, and an unbreakable cup

Multi-purpose knife and spoon

Portable washing line and detergent powder

Plug for bath or wash basin (often missing in some Asian countries)

Reading material

Business cards

Tickets, passport and visas, and extra photos for visas

Travellers cheques, bank cards (e.g. Visa, Master Card, American Express) and some cash in the local currency of your destination

International telephone calling card

Hints

Work out how much money you will need. Decide on a realistic daily allowance. Find out which credit cards are acceptable in the countries you will visit. Couples with several types of credit cards should select one card each. If your wallet is stolen you still have credit with the other card. (Carry the phone number of a friend or family member so you can phone in case your card is stolen and has to be cancelled. Problems such as these are handled better in your home town.)

Purchase travellers cheques and list their numbers in two different places. US dollar travellers cheques are acceptable in most countries. Leave a photocopy of cheque numbers with a family member or friend. You usually need your passport to cash a travellers cheque. Try to purchase some of your destination's currency before you leave home — at least enough money to get you to your accommodation, just in case the airport bank is closed. It is wise to carry a few US dollar notes in your wallet for emergencies.

Don't carry your valuables in a hand bag — wear your money and passport in a light-weight cotton money belt. Wallets in back pockets are invitations to pick-pockets. Keep cash separate from credit cards, travellers cheques and passport.

Travel with the minimum amount of luggage. In most countries you can buy what you forget. Your cabin bag should contain a change of underclothes and essential toilet items in case your other luggage goes astray.

Use a very strong suitcase — preferably one with wheels. Some fabric suitcases rip easily. Use special markings or colourful straps on your suitcase so you can identify it quickly. Start out with plenty of room in your suitcase for purchases.

Make sure your shoes have been 'broken in' and are comfortable.

If you are going on a long flight, start adjusting your sleeping schedule a few days before you leave home to help reduce 'jet lag'.

Keep your passport number and the date of issue handy — you'll need them often for completing entry forms. Photocopy your passport details and keep a copy on your travel file and at home. Carry spare passport photos for any visa applications you may need. Write in the back of your passport in pencil your current address and the name of your next of kin.

When you arrive check your valuables into the hotel safe or deposit box. It's unwise to travel with the family jewels — they are best kept in your bank at home.

On long international flights

Book in early at the airport so you have a choice of seat. If you want to read or sleep get a window seat far away from the engines. If you plan to work with papers you will have more room in an aisle seat.

Carry ear plugs, eye shades, necessary toilet items, thick travelling socks and medication in your hand luggage (with prescriptions for your medication).

Eat light meals and drink alcohol modestly. Drink plenty of water, fruit juices and non-alcoholic beverages to prevent dehydration and help reduce 'jet lag'.

Go to the toilet before meals are served. There are often long queues after the meal.

Walk around the aisles periodically to help your blood circulation.

Find out the customs restrictions before you arrive in a country. Know what imports are prohibited and how much liquor and how many cigarettes you can take in free of duty.

Never lose your temper with customs or immigration officials, however great the provocation. Polite, friendly co-operation will get you through more quickly.

In foreign countries

Ask your travel agent about local customs in the countries you will visit and respect these customs. Be sensitive to local dress codes. Shorts are often unacceptable. Women should dress appropriately in Islamic countries. Length of men's hair can cause problems, too. In some countries you do not pass food or money with your left hand.

Change your money at banks. There is usually a bank at the airport. You will often get better rates than in hotels or shops.

Get local advice on approximate taxi fares and negotiate fares before you start. In some countries where the taxi-drivers do not speak English it helps to have your destination written in the local language. Ask for a receipt for your fare — this often brings the price down.

In many countries it is not advisable to drink tap water unless you have boiled it.

Bottled water marketed by reputable firms is safer for drinking and cleaning your teeth.

Don't have ice in your drinks even in the larger hotels. It may have been made with contaminated water.

Be wary of salads and raw foods in restaurants in tropical countries. It is safer to eat cooked vegetables, and fruits you can peel yourself.

It is handy to have your own tea and coffee-making equipment. A small electric jug with a 'multi-plug'(one that can be adjusted to fit different power outlets) can be a good investment to help ensure your water is safe to drink.

Pay your hotel bill early. This gives you time to check it before you leave. Check your mini-bar bill carefully. It is often a good source of income for hotel staff.

Save enough local currency to pay your departure tax. (In some countries this tax can be paid at the hotel.)

Warnings!

Don't forget to reconfirm your flight bookings.

Don't tell people you are new in the town.

Don't keep your cash with your travellers cheques and credit cards.

Don't stand out as a tourist. Don't wear clothing that sets you apart from the locals.

Leave your travel agent's travel bag at home. On the streets it marks you as a tourist and a target for thieves.

Don't volunteer to shop for others. It can be time-consuming and stressful.

 Remember

Experienced travellers have the lightest bags.

NEVER carry parcels home as a favour for chance acquaintances! You may have many years to regret it when you reach Customs.

VISUAL AIDS

Improve your presentations

Your audience remembers about 20% of what they hear and about 80% of what they see — that's why you should use visual aids!

The simplest and easiest to use for presentations to large groups are slides and transparencies for overhead projectors. The more complicated your projector the greater the chances of things going wrong.

Slides and transparencies should be:

Simple

Easy to understand

Able to be seen by the whole audience.

Each visual aid should have a single message.

Use title phrases on charts and diagrams. For example 'Gross Income' NOT 'Graph 1'.

Ideally don't have more than six lines of writing on a transparency or more than six words per line.

Keep the lettering at least 6mm high on an overhead transparency.

" A good visual aid can save you a lot of talking."

Don't use too many visual aids. For a 20 minute talk no more than ten, preferably less. Show only the best — leave out the rest.

Rehearse your talk with your visual aids before the event.

Allow time for the audience to study each visual.

If you are using an overhead projector, switch the projector off when you want to get the audience's attention.

For details give a handout AFTER you have finished talking. If you give it out at the beginning of your talk, you will not have the full attention of your audience.

WORK

WORK

Observe basic principles

A principle is an important belief or guideline that applies anywhere and at all times.

Business leaders keep looking for new ways of doing things, but in the end they usually return to simple, fundamental principles.

Basic work principles:

1   Set your goals, objectives and targets making sure they are realistic.

2   Consult and involve staff and clients in planning.

3   List the things you have to do or the problems you have to overcome.

4   Put tasks and problems in priority order.

5   Set realistic timetables for achieving these tasks.

6   Use the 'divide and conquer' method to break up large tasks into workable bites.

7   For problems, get all the relevant information, then make fast decisions.

8   Don't procrastinate!

9   Set up good two-way information systems to keep people informed.

10   Avoid arguments as much as possible. Try to be calm, patient and cheerful.

11   Take short breaks during the day.

12   Do your best, then don't worry.

13   Relax, knowing you have done a good day's work.

14   Lead a balanced life. Remember the old adage, *"Moderation in all things".*

"We keep looking for new gurus. We try out new gimmicks. But in the end we return to basic principles."

WORK

REJOINING THE WORKFORCE

After a lengthy absence from work, boosting your confidence and self-esteem is just as important as retraining. The rules are simple for both men and women.

A five point plan for self-revival:

1   Improve your image

Smarten up your appearance. If necessary, invest in new clothes and a neat hairstyle.

Exercise regularly and make sure you have a healthy diet.

Read widely so you can discuss topical issues.

You may need lessons in deportment or help from a speech teacher.

2   Increase your confidence and self-esteem

Join organisations such as sports and cultural clubs and take on responsibilities as they arise - acting as secretary, treasurer or president.

Help with community projects, school functions or political or religious groups. Accept positions of responsibility if you are asked.

Try out new things - new hobbies, new sports, new foods. Travel to new places to meet interesting people.

Praise yourself and reward yourself for your successes and achievements.

" Be ready for an opportunity when it comes."

3   Learn new skills or update your old ones

Enrol for courses to learn new skills. Distance learning courses can be completed in your own home in your own time. It is essential to learn computer skills and to study electronic communications for most jobs today.

4 Start job hunting in earnest

Your best chance to get a job is through friends, family and acquaintances. Visit employment agencies and contact people whom you think might be able to help. Read and answer the 'situations vacant' advertisements in your local newspapers.

Don't get upset if you are not successful at the start - it's all good experience.

" If your life is free of failures you are not taking enough risks. You only fail when you give up."

5 Believe in yourself

Everyone has talent of one type or another, but most people lack the courage to make the best use of it.

If you believe in yourself you can go out and get what you want out of life. Your first step will be to build up your confidence and then with determination and persistence you should reach your goal.

When applying for jobs don't be modest. Talk about your skills and your work experiences. Be enthusiastic about your desire to join the workforce again.

Be ambitious!

 Remember

Be what you are. Become what you are capable of becoming.

WRITING ———————————————————————

Keep it simple and lively

Most people are lazy readers so if you want to write to be read, follow these simple rules.

Before you start think about your readers

What would they be interested in? Write to arouse their interest or stir their imagination.

Plan and outline

Prepare a plan and outline what you want to say. Put your main points in logical order so your ideas flow from one point to the next.

Your opening paragraph

Catch the reader's attention with a bold statement or a story. Make them want to read on.

First a rough draft

Amplify your outline — put 'flesh on the bones'. Pretend you are talking to your readers as you write. The important thing is to get your ideas down.

Polish your script

Be prepared to write and rewrite several times until it flows smoothly.

Write crisply

Use simple words and short sentences.

Make your writing lively. Use strong, positive words and active verbs.

Be enthusiastic. Share your emotions.

Write to express, not to impress. Write as you would speak. Develop your own style. (Meaning is more important than style.)

" Think about your readers before you start writing. Try to write for a specific person."

Write about people. Tell stories, relate anecdotes and share experiences.

Use dialogue. Quotation marks attract attention, so use dialogue to emphasise special points. Invent people — invent conversations to add variety to your writing.

Paragraphs

Vary the length of your paragraphs, but generally keep them short.

Lively pages

Leave plenty of white spaces to break up your text. There is nothing more daunting than a book or a report with long chapters made up of long paragraphs.

Edit...edit...edit

Remove all unnecessary words and phrases, jargon and clichés. Make sure your meanings are clear and there are no ambiguous statements. Be ruthless — chop and change and rearrange statements until your writing sounds right to your ear. Check and re-check spelling, grammar and punctuation.

Your final draft

When you are satisfied, give your draft to a colleague for comments and helpful criticism. With their fresh approach, they may find errors and omissions.

WRITING

Use non-sexist language

Writers often face a dilemma when trying to overcome problems of gender and avoid sexist language. The English language lacks a 'unisex' third person singular pronoun, so some writers use 'he/she' or 'his/her'. These are clumsy and interrupt the flow of words in a sentence especially if it has to be read aloud. Avoid them if possible but if you can't, try some of the following:

1 Use a gender-neutral term

Instead of...	write...
businessman	business executive
chairman	chairperson
fireman	fire-fighter
fisherman	fisher
foreman	supervisor
mankind	people
manpower	personnel
policeman	police officer
postman	postal worker
workman	worker
to man	to operate,

and so on....

"Remove gender from your agenda!"

2 Rewrite your statement in the plural

Instead of ... Each applicant must bring his birth certificate.

write... Applicants must bring their birth certificates.

Instead of ... Every trainer should prepare his or her visual aids.

write... All trainers should prepare their own visua

3   Address your reader directly in the second person

Instead of ...   Each person is responsible for keeping his office clean and tidy.

write...   You are responsible for keeping your office clean and tidy.

4   Replace third person singular possessive with articles

Instead of ...   Each committee member expressed his opinion.

write...   Each committee member expressed an opinion.

5   Repeat a title

Instead of ...   The Minister of Health will, at her discretion, make recommendations to the Prime Minister.

write...   The Minister of Health will, at the Minister's discretion, make recommendations to the Prime Minister.

6   Use the passive voice

If nothing else sounds right use the passive voice.

Instead of ...   Each officer presented his report.

write...   Reports were presented by each officer.

Other books by the same author:

Managing for Tomorrow

A mentor for new team leaders. A practical book showing how to carry out change; improve staff performance; avoid chaos; build teams; reduce stress; and advance your career and much more. Published in New Zealand, Singapore, , India, China, Korea and Indonesia. (290p.)

Getting Your Ideas Across

A handbook to help improve your listening, speaking, writing and meeting skills. Published in New Zealand, Great Britain, Australia and Singapore. (226p.)

Persuasive Presentations

An essential tool for planning corporate presentations. Tells you how to analyse your audience, prepare and use visual aids, speak and write persuasively, plan displays and exhibits and much more. Published in New Zealand, Australia and Singapore. (166p.)

The Trainer's Handbook

A basic international trainer's guide. Tells you how to plan and manage training. Introduces you to many training techniques with special emphasis on participative training. Published in New Zealand, Australia, Great Britain, USA, Singapore and Indonesia. (135p.)

Survival Skills for New Managers

Tells you how to start managing. Takes you back to the basics and is full of hints from top managers. Published in New Zealand, Australia, Singapore, Great Britain, Hungary, Serbia, China, South Africa. (179p.)

New Horizons

A motivational book for people changing careers; retiring early; facing redundancy; retiring to the work force or seeking international work. Written with the help of the New Zealand Employment Service. (112p.)

These simple practical books are written in global English. We have publishers in sixteen countries. For further details and a brochure giving current prices contact the publisher:

MOSS ASSOCIATES Ltd

7 Dorset Way, Wadestown, Wellington 6001, NEW ZEALAND

Phone/ Fax (04) 472 8226

Notes

Notes